FOSTERING

per

report

1990s

Also by Diana Davenport

Adoption and the Coloured Child
One-Parent Families: A Practical Guide to Coping

FOSTERING:
the inside view

Diana Davenport

COLUMBUS BOOKS
LONDON

First published in Great Britain in 1989 by
Columbus Books Limited
19–23 Ludgate Hill
London EC4M 7PD

British Library Cataloguing in Publication Data

Davenport, Diana
    Fostering: the inside view.
    1. Children. Foster care
    I. Title
    362.7'33

ISBN 0-86287-887-X

Typeset in Palatino by Selectmove Limited

Printed and bound by The Guernsey Press, Guernsey, CI

Contents

Introduction

Ashley is getting through his second year in prison. Arson with intent to endanger lives. James, back on his first leave from the Royal Greenjackets, boasts about losing his virginity. Brian, trouble-maker and fidget, rings from school saying he's won the shield for 'most helpful boy in house'. Georgina emerges tentatively from sulky resignation and seems to enjoy slapping emulsion paint on the kitchen walls. Roy reverts, if temporarily, to his days in psychiatric hospital and has a mammoth go of hysteria outside school. Ben, 90% paralysed from midriff down, scrapes a livid hole in his senseless foot. Tom, nine, superior as ever, informs those of us assembled for tea that 'dwarfism, of course, is usually caused by the pituitary gland not working properly'. (We had seen a minute man at the newsagent's in town earlier.) Hugh, as every day, keeps up his falsetto chatter until one's ears ring.

Statements stabbed out at random from my fostering day, so that this ill-balanced list may cast an early shadow over any illusion that fostering involves sugar-sweet little cherubs, problem-free, grateful for shelter and the love of a new Mummy and Daddy. In real life, well-mannered cherubs avoid coming into care. It's the miscreants and misfits who tend to find themselves struggling to adapt to a second set of parents. And a third, fourth, fifth and more, if the dice land against them.

What I'm trying to get over, fast, is that fostering is mostly jolly hard work. It shreds our nerves; causes us to bite our tongues, hide our feelings and tactfully close both eyes and ears. One of the last remaining unpaid jobs, it certainly has what people call rewards, yet it is no venture for the soppy-hearted. Your mattresses will be ruined, your talc shaken like snow all down the landing, your perfume spilled. The refrigerator will not only be raided, but its door will be left open after the pillage. Money will be pinched; undesirable friends will be brought home; Radio One will blare; screwdrivers, scissors, razor blades and banker's cards will vanish without trace. So will your socks. And nobody will ever own up.

Don't read any more unless you possess a bomb-proof sense of altruism, a stubborn drive and an unconditional view of love.

Fostering can be divided broadly into two disparate slots. For many couples and, more rarely, single people, the addition of one or more long-term fostered children to their existing family might be referred to as a philanthropic top-up; a once-and-for-all foray into expansion.

Others, myself included, take to fostering in a more capacious manner; sometimes indeed with a positive flourish, and wholly open-ended. Such families, mine included, may well consist of one's own children, whether by birth or adoption, and permanent foster children, as well as those who come in and go out of the domestic circle as short-term needs arise.

The long-term ones, who become as it were grafted on, generally function to a standard pattern, though protected by the legislative arm of The Child Care Act, 1980. In cases where parents have taken on their extras as infants, pressures in the future will in most cases be few. Material and emotional wear-and-tear should fall into the same bracket as in any run-of-the-mill family. Patterns of speech, mannerisms and rules requiring conformity to the family's moral code will be laid down without effort, without overt teaching. Yes, we do have to mention this – and if you really stir your priorities you may find that it does matter to you how, say, he holds his fork. Clashes of temperament may be no more difficult than those within the normal parents/children set-up.

On the other hand, fostering is, in the nature of things, disruptive; disruptive to both the fosterers and the fostered. We may, when the light shines in the right direction, think it isn't or that it won't be; but it is. As foster parents we are going beyond the tribal norm; we are offering ourselves on the do-gooders' altar; we are knowingly spreading ourselves more thinly in the context of our nuclear family. We are taking on the unknown.

'A child is a child is a child . . . ' may be sweetly voiced by the open-hearted earth-mother eager to bare her bosom to the waifs and strays of this uneasy world. But put this blanket of social piety to the practical test and she'll most likely change key to 'a child is a monster, a humanized bulldozer, a devious manipulator, a brick wall', or yet 'a shrinking violet, a frightened rabbit, an utterly flattened small person'.

In the trade, that is the welfare profession as a whole, all these kinds of children are currently referred to as being damaged; they are, like poor little bruised plums left over from the shake-up of a market stall.

Most children coming into care have problems yet, with the closing of so many Children's Homes they require placement with a foster family. Whether stemming from conditions at home such as separation from parents, mental or moral or physical bashing, inadequate or feeble parenting and so on, or from the child himself who may have a mental or physical handicap, many behave in a grossly unacceptable way and their dilemmas are incapable of solution within their own family. Were it otherwise, then grannies, aunties, godparents or any one of an assortment of other kindly folk (even, in more elevated circles, hired nannies), would long ago have offered their own hearths and hearts, thus obviating the need for the welfare services to set their wheels turning.

Let incipient fosterers realize that, more often than not, a placement involves the child and his family, troubles and all. A willingness to open your arms and dispense love is not enough. You have to give over long hours to harrowing accounts of other people's lives; their awful wives, their unhinged husbands, their damp and crumbling homes, their ulcers and veins, their older children who are pregnant, are rabid punk, are ugly with glue, are too lazy to wash a dinner plate, are in youth custody.

You are also exposed to lives so overflowing with real anguish that they make you beam up a prayer; mortally sick partners, irrevocable handicaps, heads beaten against brick walls to no effect, decisions only reached after much thought on nerves made raw at the prospect of parting with a child. The real stories behind such separations seldom stop short of tears.

Understandably, children of both considered partings and those more thoughtlessly reached are not inclined to respond to any substitute caring with overt gratitude. The children we receive, by and large, see no reason to show thanks; they do not want to be in our houses; they do not like our food ('I never touches that sort of thing'); they do not appreciate our prissy manners nor our leaning towards what may well be seen as the know-all syndrome.

Don't forget that, at the same time as making this adjustment, the child is also fighting with the terrible grief of losing his real home, with a sense of injustice, even with a richly-layered hatred towards us. For how does he know, in his ignorance of The Child Care Act, 1980, that we did not engineer this all-change for our own gratification?

Later on, of course, given that a particular child remains in the longer term as part of our family and is not too deeply scarred by his past – affection can be decently reciprocated and many of his attitudes begin to fit in with our own. That happens when fostering comes out of the wood and we can begin to ease off the vigilance, can all start to enjoy the expansion into big family living.

Fosterers must also be prepared to face the reality of the wholly rejected child; the little matchgirls of this world, with no interested relatives, no memory of maternal warmth nor of a home acquired by birth. Such a child has no experience of dispensing fondness in any guise, nor any motivation towards making an attachment. The linchpin of life becomes 'my social worker', a professionally concerned person, paid for the job, whose place it is to keep as leakproof a roof as possible over this young person's head, and to sweep the minefield of her future. Not infrequently, alas, that social worker is entangled in the business of keeping this emotionally-blunted child out of trouble, or of plotting her removal from one fraught situation to a hoped-for better one. It's a tough proposition: for the carer as well as for the child.

This introduction is intended as a caution, a putter-off or a sorter-out, a damper on passions roused by advertisements for fostering one reads in *The Guardian*, designed to attract the attention of schoolteachers, clerics and other likely candidates. Adjectives freely made use of, and which should be taken with a pinch of salt, include impish, mischievous, strong-willed, boisterous and, a real warning light, disturbed. These words serve as euphemisms for unbiddable, plain naughty, destructive, loud and unpredictable. Nevertheless, if you would-be-gooders are truly set on the winding path to fostering, let me show you the way – pointing out pleasures and pitfalls, the heights of bureaucracy to be scaled and the depths of human misery to be understood.

CHAPTER 1

Children who need fostering

Whether it be myth or reality I don't know, but there is a popularly held theory among laymen, largely borne out by fact, that problems of (mis)behaviour, character, criminal and unsociable tendencies and such-like are not infrequently passed down from one generation to another. This belief has been held for as long as our system has thrived. That the misdemeanours of forebears shall be visited upon successive generations is quoted today with as much fervency as it was in the past. That bad blood will out is still seriously postulated by parents who are disappointed in the outcome of an adopted child or, come to that, of a long-term fostered one. Nor is it unknown for a parent to feel less than satisfied with the direction taken by a child of his own making. The old, old battle of heredity jostling for first place against environment. A pre-programmed destiny? All parents, including those from the upper crust, will from time to time actually despair of their own offspring. The silk purse has seemingly bred a pig's ear. The high-flying barrister whose 16-year-old stole grandmother's silver and flogged it at Hatton Garden admitted that he had always felt the boy to be bad. Was father the chicken or the egg? Who, once the kick against self and society has gathered momentum, can unravel the threads of cause and effect? The actual dislike between parent and recalcitrant child destroys rational analysis. Often early mischievousness, disapproved of, runs on, via spite, into outright and deliberate naughtiness, into the breaking of social mores and into the abuse of both the law and the family's expectations. The heat generated by a predetermined flow of events can result in rejection which is welcomed as a relief by all; it is a tragedy turned on its head.

A child with this behaviour pattern, beyond parental control and in nine cases out of ten the pain of long-suffering schoolteachers, could well be obliged to cool his adolescent heels in care over the later teenage years. This boy and his likes are not favourites of the fostering fraternity. Too much of a risk, disruptive, cocky and presenting a ghastly example to the other more vulnerable children of the family. He is seldom taken on with relish.

In many cases such a child, committed subconsciously to self-destruction, has long been singled out from his siblings and made the scapegoat for parental transgressions; the sins of the fathers again. The ex-colonial tea-planter who took sexual advantage of his somewhat backward son, swearing him to secrecy, rejecting him when the boy gathered up the gumption to say 'no', created an ambience of discomfort which tipped over into persecution. Mother, probably the weaker parent, either did not, or chose not to, see what was going on in the child's room when he'd been sent up to bed.

Getting one's own back in the form of kicking against ethical standards escalates into wholesale and multilateral family distress. The child will do his own thing, go his own way, express his own self-centred opinions, yet he has, like children the world over, merely resigned himself to the mould created by the sickness of his environment and confirmed by his innate predilections. His predictable route into care looks like being equated with taking the rap.

Situational rejection such as outlined above has always been with us. In times past a child born to a supposed witch, sorcerer or evil-eye was ostracized, while in many areas of the world, even today, a baby delivered with a noticeable physical abnormality may be abandoned and left to the weather. Twins may be seen as abnormal in some regions. These children are marked as outsiders from the moment they are born. Some have the good fortune, good, I mean, considering the circumstances, to survive time-honoured superstitions of their native traditions by being found. Such a one was J, a skinny infant, estimated to be around eight months old, weighing only a few pounds, with an unrepaired hare-lip and cleft palate. Found in a Hong Kong street, she was taken to an orphanage from where, by the time she was three, moves had been made with a view to adoption towards a firm fostering placement in Britain. She has been my daughter for many years now.

However, such international placements have in recent years become less popular. The real 'take me or I'll most likely die' children of raw poverty, born in areas where famine or natural disasters make survival chancey, to say the least, are now thought best left where they are. The air-lift, after all, might drop a bag of wheat. The doctor who covers thousands of square miles on unlikely transport might come. Father might find work. The crops might bear fruit. Mother might not conceive again for a bit. Pigs might fly.

Everyone is, naturally, allowed to hold their own opinion on international placements. The movement, backed by the voluntary societies, flourished as the green bay throughout the 1960s and was very much bound up in the belief that the refugee problem could be solved for all time. But this proved a naive attitude.

Many organizations, Project Vietnam Orphans among them, pursued their ideals into the children's futures. The new parents were reminded that, should the child show an interest in a field which could be explored in the country of her birth, then the possibility of her (less often his) return to that country of birth should be encouraged. Perhaps some of those 'sixties children have done so. What I am certain of is that, so far as is traceable, these lost, abandoned and starving young things, brought from the far corners of a harsher world than ours a quarter of a century and more ago, have done well in the West. They did not sustain a culture shock of lasting hurt; have bonded with families poles apart from those of their origins; have grown up, entered the ranks of the workers; have married and borne children. Moreover, and contrary to the self-consciousness about colour rammed into the present generation of trans-racial placements, these first children to be integrated have, on the whole, shown no inclination to bleat about the shade of their skin or the contours of their physiognomy.

No voluntary organizations involve themselves in this type of rescue transplantation now. Only a few individual stalwarts, determined to salvage a child by dint of courage and without sponsorship, return from one of the impoverished regions of the world with small human beings who, with no future in their own land, have most likely been bought by these modern philanthropists or by the desperate childless.

The pressures of too much to do and too little training in what we've now come to call basic skills can cause a parent to cry not only 'help' but also 'halt!'. This is the one who has slipped through the net during the time when a change of course could have been foreseen. The professionals, doctors, health visitors and welfare workers alike, have missed the warning signs. Shedding the load can become the only option if the mother is to maintain even minimal control. The last straw has to be withdrawn from the overburdened and inadequate.

Say father is in prison for fraudulently drawing what's known as 'the Social' while actually working as a cleaner at the bus garage. Mother is driving herself to keep tabs on the four children aged five, four, three and two with which an incomplete understanding of contraceptive methods has landed her. Child no. 5, a poor physical specimen and a persistent crier, has earned little love and is offered no more than his mother feels to be his just desserts.

She had asked for an abortion when 2½ months pregnant but had been encouraged by her GP to soldier on in the certainty that once she'd held him (the infant, not the doctor) in her arms, she would love him. But the fifth-time mother hadn't done so. She'd felt nothing, not even despair. She took this unwanted luggage home, fed it and kept it cleanish; she shut her ears to the thin cry and got on with her other commitments.

Babies being the time-grabbers they are, no. 5 objected to this indifference. The thin cry found body; the little limbs flailed in anger. With time, his sharp milk teeth were put to good use, biting both the hand that fed him and any morsel of sibling flesh on offer. The neighbours, ever mindful, became concerned at the ever-growing intensity of yelling and counter-yelling. Inevitably, somebody split and, not a moment too soon, 'the welfare' eased its way gently into that chaotic home and offered balm. The mother, her man still away, was worn to a shred, uninterested in housekeeping, motherhood and all things culinary. No. 5, she contended, had been the end.

Sympathy and understanding offered by a middle-aged (mother figure?) social worker served to open the floodgates. No.5 had never been wanted; she'd been made to have him in spite of pleading to the contrary; he'd been a wingeing, aggressive infant all through his first year and had embarked upon his second with mobile gusto. She only wished to God, she said, that he'd never been born.

The toddler was removed, to his mother's open relief, under Section 2 (Voluntary Care) of The Child Care Act. This erstwhile cuckoo in the nest is seldom seen by any natural relative, although visiting is by no means restricted. A difficult boy, craving the love he never experienced yet unable to recognize it when it comes his way, he has taken an unusually long time to settle into the foster family which is commited to providing him with a long-term home.

A see-saw of 'love you, love you not' is not uncommon among some more lively single mothers who see their children as a tie which prevents the outside world and its attendant glitter getting in ... the grass is always greener ...

A girl of 25 is stuck with a boisterous six-year-old and a toddler. Her man left her for pastures new when the baby was a month old. Paternity was an open question in both cases and there was no obligation either to provide for or take an interest in the children. For the two-and-a-half years following the breakdown of what had been a relatively stable relationship, a definite pattern of positive/negative mothering repeated itself. Overt neglect followed by relief foster care followed by a restoration period repeated themselves at a rate of about three complete cycles a year. There was no real contact with grandparents save in the role of critics. Other relatives, living in the vicinity, refrained from offering practical help but not from throwing mud.

This young woman, not cut out, perhaps, for life at the kitchen sink, burned the candle at both ends. By the nature of her predicament she was lonely, and a series of assorted lads, two or three of whom the children were expected to call Daddy, paid court. Mother was seldom up in time to take the older child to school, while the younger was more often than not still in bed at midday.

Though the school and the social services department were concerned for the welfare (not safety) of these children, it could not be denied that the mother was at least fulfilling the minimal duties of feeding and washing. Indeed their smart appearance when going out was of great importance to her.

Lack of stimulation and significant neglect are hard to prove and in taking any child into care the facts must ring sounder than mere speculation. Thus it was not until the children were actually known to have been left alone in the house overnight that a concerned neighbour provided the cue for the social services to move in.

As it turned out this was in fact what the mother had, rather more than subconsciously, hoped for. She contended that she had no life of her own and was entitled to some freedom for herself to both make and sustain relationships. She was desolate. She was victimized. The neighbours made her existence unbearable and called her a whore. The children never left her alone, were forever whining for sweets or Coke or for her to go to the shop and get a new video. She didn't know if she loved them. They'd do better with other people. She thought she'd move right away, without them, and make a new start.

The good social services, understanding the confusion, dissatisfaction and inertia and seeing that she had reached breaking-point, stepped in for the nth time with respite care. (Respite care is short-term, a life-saver or a breather.) This temporary relief became elasticated, stretched almost imperceptibly into the longer term and ultimately reached a pretty satisfactory arrangement of shared care. The children stayed with a foster mum throughout the week, went to school and were cared for in every respect. Mother had them each weekend, was able to sustain her affection for 48 hours and to keep the link with earlier days.

This is a situation, not all that unusual, which obviously calls for much patient harmony between foster family and natural mother. The element of possessiveness, which ought to be eschewed yet is inescapable in most full-time, long-term placements, lacks an edge; the willingness to share events, achievements and occasions with Mum is important. Sometimes the load-bearing foster parent must give way to sail when, for instance, tickets for events like the school concert, pantomime or carol service are limited. In such a placement the fosterers come second – and ought to remember it.

Virtuous people with haloes, such as those who have never put a foot wrong, never been tempted to break the rules or to wriggle out of a moral commitment, find it absolutely impossible to understand how a parent can willingly relinquish a child to be cared for as part of another family. This uncharitable sentiment is never more pronounced, even among relatives of those intimately concerned with the decision, than where a birth-damaged or congenitally handicapped baby is the central character.

The question can of course be answered hypothetically by ourselves or the childless or the parents of normally developing offspring. On the one side, we have, 'I could never in a million years bring myself to part with any baby I bore, whatever the changes it would bring into our own lives'. On the other, 'I could never face keeping a child who was seriously abnormal. I wouldn't have the patience or the stomach to go through with it. And of course it would be mightily unfair to the rest of the family.' We therefore have the larger section of society showing compassion for the infant, born by nature's standards imperfect, coupled with a practical willingness to rear such a child and draw out all that is possible in the way of potential.

But that leaves a still sizable group of parents, or future parents, having apparently thought out their opinions as to their suitability/unsuitability and (let's face it) their moral objections to rear any handicapped child they may have brought, or be about to bring, into the world.

It's easy to criticize, to throw verbal stones, to set sentiment above harsh reality. But few if any new parents, faced with a baby born with severe abnormalities, opt for home or away without deep soul-searing deliberation. About three-quarters, however, do decide in favour of looking after these special children themselves. These brave stalwarts, accepting all that fate has laid at their feet, know the odds and accept them. They are, in general, pledging their troth to decades of loving service, to recurring periods of anxiety and to above-average strain. Maternal/paternal stress can and does affect the entire fabric of a family. It is well known that such a household may, if offered no relief over the years, become fragmented.

A highish number of marriages, within which a demanding handicapped child is reared, do come to grief through sheer strain.

Equally courageous, yet in quite a different way, are those parents who, having looked into their emotional, physical and material resources, feel that they cannot cope. They know with bedrock certainty that bringing up their child, with his handicaps, would neither be in his best interest nor in theirs. In rare cases a parent takes against a newborn infant who does not conform to the pattern of flawless presentation. More frequently a shock-wave of indifference numbs reality and this can, if protracted, lead to a decision not to keep the child.

Whatever the reason for making the decision, we, the foster parents of such children, must not judge those who, with undoubted anguish, have given up their handicapped into care. We will, thanks to human nature, probably be quizzed by acquaintances and receive gratuitous opinions by the frankly nosy. Always, when thus assailed, change into a lower gear and calmly manoeuvre the conversation sideways. The child's parents did what they did for the best; their reasons are no business of ours, nor of our neighbours. They have in all probability gone through hell; have been got at by relatives and whispered about by their neighbours. We have undertaken to nurture a handicapped child by choice. We are being paid a generous maintenance allowance for doing so. With luck we just might be offered occasional relief care. We slot into a different league altogether.

Our present divorce rate of approximately one-quarter of all marriages is unprecedented. About two-thirds of all divorced couples have children. In the vast majority of cases it is the mother who both wants and gets care and control of any offspring, while the father holds, jointly with her, equal custody.

However, over 7,000 children each year are received into care by way of court orders following domestic or matrimonial proceedings. Sometimes neither parent is, solo, considered to be a fit person to be given unsupported care. Sometimes neither parent actually wants to have the children live with them. Sometimes the children themselves, in opposition to their parents' wishes, and with the full backing of a court welfare officer, decide of their own free will not to reside with either father or mother. Thus children can be switched from the shadow of matrimonial mayhem to the relative tranquillity of a foster home. Many will be nervous, suspicious, untrusting, fearful of the very concept of family. Others may be over-bumptious; privy to the rows, bitterness and bizarre jockeying of grown-ups who, once in love, have fallen heavily out of it. They will know it all and, on the rebound from affection lost, will be wary of accepting other affections at face value.

From these direct casualties of separation and divorce we move on to failures of later relationships. I refer to the classic catastrophe of the wicked stepparent. Two or three decades ago the advent of a stepparent largely followed widowhood. Where a child has been bonded emotionally, has loved his absent parent, he is going enormously to resent the replacement whom the remaining parent presents. Since the mythical days of Cinderella the incoming adult has been branded as bad. The child's peers may well commiserate, add fuel to the emotional fire, actually encourage dissatisfaction and unhappiness.

In fact, once a child is beyond the age of around five years, a second marriage or partnership is likely to spark off troubles varying from absolutely excruciating down to mildly sore. The nature of the beast is to protest at change. The new mother of a ready-made family, bursting with good intentions, anxious to show affection, more than willing to ease in slowly and make allowances, can herself be made miserable by a hostile stepchild. If that hostility is not dissipated, or indeed cannot be eased, the father sometimes has to make a choice between the new wife and the child(ren). (Likewise new husband/mother.) Such a choice is desperately hard to make but, in practical terms, is often weighted against the child.

The stepchild, or it might be better to call him the opted-out stepchild, becomes a foster-child. Largely through his own overt rejection of change at home, his dejection stems from perfectly valid reasons derived from deep-felt mourning. Loss by death and loss by disappearance are synonymous to most children. The child who distances himself from his roots by self-propulsion is sad, angry, accusative and difficult. He is a piece of modern flotsam well established on the fostering scene and is likely to stay there for all time.

Father is undoubtedly not very bright. He slipped the net of school, is unemployable and, though gentle by nature and a thoroughly nice man, is hopelessly lost now that his wife has been stricken with inoperable cancer. There is one child, a girl of twelve, of average intelligence, but given to what both parents term rebellion. The atmosphere at home is fraught; there is a terrible realization of unfairness, of fear, and of love. The woman who has for years held everything together, has managed the housekeeping brilliantly, has encouraged her child of a husband to read, to write, to struggle with the quick crossword in their daily paper, is going to die. No doubt about it. Sensible even in her anger at the illness, the mother knows that her daughter will not be able to continue to live at home. The daughter, impatient with her father's slowness and drawn to the glamour she imagines she glimpses on the other side of the social rainbow, agrees with her mother's approach to the social services. The girl settles with apparent satisfaction in a foster family where she is one of three girls. Access is open and she generally opts to spend alternate weekends at her parents' flat. This pattern will in all probability continue after her mother's death.

Contrary to widespread belief there are extremely few children in care solely on account of homelessness. At any one time, there are less that 250 placements directly attributable to, say, eviction. So long as all else is satisfactory families really are kept together whatever the inadequacies of their housing. Look at the thousands who make their home in one room or who live in the close confines of bed and breakfast. Yet, in spite of tenant-orientated legislation, there are still those rare occasions where parents with young children are thrown out onto the streets.

Some are shown the door after a row with parents/grandparents or other friends/relatives with whom they have roosted. Others, come the spring, find they must move from a holiday cottage which has served as home over the preceding months. The landlord may be in a quandary because he has paying visitors moving in for, perhaps, Easter week, and others booked thereafter. The little family, at the end of their tenancy, have found no other accommodation within their means. Both the social services and the housing department have told them to stay put regardless, that in law they cannot be turned out, that they must play for time and, if pressed, threaten to take the landlord to court. This universal and monstrous advice, dished out daily in myriad council offices, constitutes one of the main reasons why private tenancies are so hard to come by. Courteous persuasion and an appeal both to reason and for help can often conjure up alternative accommodation. In fact, very rarely does a precipitous bunk result in children experiencing, howsoever briefly, life in a foster home.

The need for temporary fostering may arise with non-conformist families, such as the travellers and bus people because of the weather. Caught in straitened circumstances and a bitter spell, or in torrential and continuous rain which invades tent, teepee or motor vehicle, these parents could be obliged, on no other grounds than lack of warm and dry shelter, to allow their children to be taken into care for a time while awaiting sun, warm winds and a settled forecast.

These travelling children are quite an experience for the foster family. Enormously self-assured and with a wide and slightly off-beat vocabulary, they are certain of their rights, up to date with the workings and manoeuvrability of the DHSS, able to stand level with adults.

It is true though that the vast majority of foster parents work through their entire career without catching so much as a fleeting glimpse of a 100% homeless child.

At the other end of the scale, alas, come the 41,000-plus children received into care as a result of action taken against parent(s) because of ill-treatment or neglect. We have all, over the years, been shattered periodically by the pathetic little case histories of this or that child coming into our homes. The small girl tremulous with fear, with uncertainty, with self-deprecation. The 'dirty' child and the one unable to speak. These are the sons and daughters of harsh or short-tempered or irrationally ambivalent parents. They might also be the children of exhausted human beings, past the end of any tether, unable to cope for another single moment.

Cruelty in action, as any of us may read in the press almost any day of the week, exists behind the house doors of this street and that throughout the land. The NSPCC is busier now than ever; more actions are brought against parents and stepparents and co-habitees; yet there seems no way of stopping this domination of brute strength over the frailty of childhood.

Who are these bruisers, the so-called batterers in our midst? Most might be said to stem from that stratum where relative poverty, semi-literacy and unemployment are taken for granted and are considered to be unchangeable. With her man about the house all day, perhaps the mother finds her natural say over the children's discipline and routine threatened. She might be accused of putting the children first. Jealousy or irritation or the sheer ubiquitousness of the toys beneath the feet, the noise assailing the ears, the demands and questions repeated and repeated; all or any of these could tip a harassed parent into acts of of cruelty in the short term. Tragically, they find that abuse, once found to be effective, can all too easily be repeated over the long term and become unstoppable, downright damaging. The mother, driven to making a choice between losing her man or letting things slip, will over and over again turn a blind eye to the contusions and broken skin, the broken ribs and even greater obscenities. She has become conditioned.

Then there are the children with children. Most years one or two 11-year-olds give birth to babies of their own. Most years three times as many 12-year-olds similarly produce tiny sons or daughters. By thirteen the number has quadrupled; by fifteen the statisticians no longer raise an eyebrow.

Children remain in care until the age of eighteen, so it isn't difficult to conclude that at least some of these child-mothers are already in Community Homes or with foster parents when their own children are conceived and/or delivered. Their infants are born into care by virtue of the uterus in which they matured. Mother and baby are a package, and assistance, supervision and friendly guidance must take account of both children together.

Some under-age mothers come into care as a result of their pregnancies and find themselves out on a limb and dealing with social services for the first time, perhaps as late as after the baby's arrival. Whatever the setting, it is inevitable that a cross-section of these girls, plus their babies, are placed in foster families. Though not a new phenomenon, society's attitude to it has changed. Until the end of the 1950s there was a stigma attached to illegitimacy. The child-mother more often spent her six weeks between parturition and the infant's adoption in the limbo of a mother-and-baby home than within the more intimate atmosphere of a foster family.

The Swinging Sixties brought the pill and sexual liberation, and also a more tolerant public attitude toward illegitimacy and the first real gift of option in respect of adoption. Girls complete with babies (in utero or in full voice) began to feature on the placement figures in the true sense of parenting within a grafted family. Many still stoically opted to give their child away, but the majority chose to shoulder the responsibility of rearing their baby who would not have to suffer from any legal disabilities by being born out of wedlock.

All the children in our secondary schools, whether comprehensive, public or private, are at risk. Loss of virginity no longer makes news for either gender; pregnancy may stir a ripple or two. The early weeks may be fraught with fear for the immediate future – tomorrow, next week, the end of the year; for telling those outside the immediate circle of school cronies. Some keep their condition secret from parents for months. A diminutive proportion of teenage girls manage to keep going to full term, when they either crack or go into labour alone, sometimes in terrifying circumstances: their own bedroom, some secluded outdoor spot, or even a hospital lavatory. An average of 21,000 unmarried under-18-year-olds give birth each year; about 700 of these deliveries result in stillbirth.

If you talk to secondary school pupils it becomes apparent that, while most do stick to the confines of the generous margin in which sex itself is not out of the question, a smaller number see no harm in a girl's becoming a very young single mother if, they say, that's what she really wants.

'It's her body and she has a right to use it as she likes. If she's fond of the boy, or gets caught out, then she's entitled to choose a baby rather than an abortion. Nobody can force you into anything you don't want to do these days.' This is the view of one mature and sexually experienced 13-year-old, who, not having any leanings towards examinations or a career herself, would like to plan for her own baby at around fifteen or sixteen.

It is not only the children themselves who feel this way. I have known grannies in this situation to state phlegmatically and unsentimentally that 'it'll give her something to do, won't it?' Granny, in many cases, is a mere slip of a thing around thirty-five.

The babies' fathers could be schoolboys or older youths or men friends, whether conceptions are deliberately sought or fall into the don't-care-one-way-or-the-other category. Pregnancy, with at least a thread of romance, a knowledge of risk and an added thrill of beating grown-ups at their own game, bestows a certain kudos. It adds stature as well as potential girth.

Quite a different state of affairs is the pregnancy engendered by a man who has 'taken advantage' of the girl or where it is the result of incest; or, though more rarely within this age group, by rape. Abortion, in these cases, will generally hush up the transgression. However, we know that some girls will hide a pregnancy either through fear or because, whoever the baby's father might be, she wants to have it.

One 16-year-old, having the previous year produced a daughter by a contemporary, conceived again by her mother's boy-friend, a middle-aged man who, she

27

conceded, 'had her' while her mother was out at work. This pregnancy, owing to the delicate nature of the relationship, was hidden from the family until close to term. The atmosphere at home became thick with argument and accusation and the girl was more or less ostracized there. It was far too late for termination and, after the girl had been delivered at home, she and her two babes were moved out to temporary accommodation. Not surprisingly, the second infant was rejected by both his mother and his grandmother. Real neglect ensued and all three were later placed together in foster care.

Couples, or singles, prepared to take in either pregnant girls or mini-families have to come to terms with present day pressures and the moral climate among modern schoolchildren. Bear in mind that some young people, and some from a very early age, are exposed to explicit television and video films at home. Sex education, right or wide of the mark according to individual opinion, can titillate an enquiring mind and actually precipitate sexual encounters which might in other circumstances have been circumnavigated. Advertising, pop culture, parental failure to veil their own sexual activities or to set down guidelines all influence the young adolescent to behave in ways that he/she imagines to be adult.

The child who has not had much notice taken of her finds that pregnancy draws attention for a while. Somebody, perhaps several somebodies, seem to care, to run round after little comforts, to offer suggestions and solutions and generally treat her as special. The very child in the womb shows this girl to be experienced, interesting or (and just as good as far as the new attention goes), fast. Or more pejoratively, no better than she should be. So she sticks her stomach out the more.

The expectant teenager is awkward to fit into an otherwise innocent foster family. The mother and father can rationalize the situation, can tread carefully, can offer what's needed at the right time and in the correct manner which must be not too soft, not too hard. They can coax out the worries and pour oil on the choppy waters. Younger members of the family, those past the age of innocent acceptance, are not yet able to assess fairly what is, to them, a fascinating condition.

I have had in this house, as an emergency placement, a child with a two-year-old son. My two eldest fostered teenagers, a boy and a girl, were both older than this little mother and on her arrival were consumed with interest. How had it happened? Where? (Behind the football club.) Who was he? (A pupil on the run from a school for maladjusted boys.) Did it hurt? (Not going to tell you.) The birth, silly. (Oh, awful, bloody awful, and they left me on this slab sort of bed so long I thought I was meant to be dead.) And how on earth did she break it to her Mum, her school, her nice old Gran?

When they grew familiar with the facts the whole thing began to pall. The child's child was quite a brat; very noisy and demanding and destructive and not biddable at all. He ate nothing but Rice Krispies and chocolate drops. He would lisp obscenities. He would scream fortissimo for anything he fancied by night or by day.

The child-mother kept relative peace by plentiful supplies of the aforesaid chocolate buttons until the point of sickness was reached. Attempting to steer this girl along the path of happy parenthood was, after her two-year false start, like dropping a minute pebble into Niagara. The house was vibrant with their presence. It was not an easy time and we were all relieved when more permanent sheltered accommodation was found for them.

On the other hand, a mid-teens mother coming straight from maternity hospital with a brand new infant, ready to embark upon parenthood, still under the awesome aura of the birth experience, can be a lovely addition to a foster family. She is genuinely eager to learn, to do right by her baby, to put herself second. A newly-born in the house is no threat to existing fostered children; he presents a learning opportunity for them, an exercise in gentleness and frailty as well as in day-to-day management.

If asked whether you are willing to take a child and her baby too, think about it very carefully. Such a placement demands a great deal of your time and counselling. The little mother, in addition to being a child, has already experienced what is perhaps the most emotionally uplifting/harrowing/thrilling experience of the human adult. She has punished her body, may have ruined her short-lived figure, has totally changed her status in the eyes of not only her immediate family and neighbours but in the world as well. She may not yet recognize her new image and almost certainly she will not yet realize, in practical terms, the implication of changes in responsibility which motherhood brings with it.

Both of you will have a lot to learn together. Unlike the others she will not go off to school, or to a YTS job, or indeed out to play. If not exactly under your feet, she will be about the place and needing your ears, eyes and intellect. It's important to meet and make mental notes before agreeing to accept a mother with her child as part of the family, even though her proposed stay may be short. Character, temperament, outlook and malleability are not that difficult to assess. Get to know her. Talk to her woman to woman rather than down to her. Let a bit of yourself out as well as hoovering up personal gems from her. Strain for any little threads of common ground: try to see her as a woman, not a child. Will her to accept your friendship and warmth; and be ready to accept hers. She is vulnerable, has myriad problems all of which need to be resolved pretty quickly. This baby of hers, however and whyever begotten, has altered her life irrevocably, even if she decides ultimately to give him for adoption.

Foster mothers past their prime, a trifle faded and perhaps no longer able to slide into a size twelve skirt, do sometimes find that the teenaged mum (like some teenagers who are not mothers) will make a beeline for the foster father. This could cause a small ripple. Carry it off with a light-hearted acceptance and know that it is all part of growing up. It takes more than a fifteen-year-old to rock a stable marriage.

Hero-worship of this nature may be turned on its head to effect therapy: foster father may be able to get through where others fail. He could well be the one to open her up to the whole family and thus embark upon separating current emotions, baby and all, from long-term practicalities.

There have been cases where teenagers' attentions have proved too much for comfort. Foster mother, if she's not the right sort to smile at this type of thing, could take umbrage, feel threatened, even begin to be uncharitable. Father might, of course, take casual flight from unsought flattery, could opt out of any participation in that particular fostering scheme, could bring to an end the whole concept of sharing a family.

So, think about it carefully, ridiculous though it may seem, before you agree to offer accommodation to a maturing girl. Be ready for it, at least as one of the possibilities.

Be ready too to be approached by grandparents of the new baby. They may be desperate to bring him up or eager that, for his own good, he be given the chance to become the adopted son of some well-off couple who would give him the best that money can buy. In their way they are hurt or angry or knocked flat by the event. They are desperate to love their grandchild and may oppose their daughter's wish to part with him. Grandparents come in every shape and form just as other human beings do. Listen and commiserate and lend your shoulder, but do not advise. It is not your business to do so. Grandparents have no right in law over the lives of their grandchildren, not even when the mothers of those grandchildren are under age.

Fathers of your smallest paying guest may also turn up on your doorstep. Fresh-faced schoolboys who look as if butter wouldn't melt; nattily-dressed crooks who eye the candlesticks; nervous married men able only to whisper; or poor old broken-down things. I've seen them all; half-proud, half-terrified. One came to 'settle' with a wad of grubby notes, another swore everlasting fidelity while desperately making for the door, a third cried tears of bewilderment. The assorted men and boys will in all likelihood tell you their side of the story over tea and the remains of supper. They may ache for your soothing and forgiving words as they fork in the bubble-and-squeak. They are part of the scene, yet few will stick to what might be termed their honourable duties. Indeed, one of the smoother of my various girls' suitors gave her the second baby while I was digging the celery trench one bright spring day.

Nowadays, of course, it is more than likely that your young mother will have been told about the relative simplicities of contraception before she comes to stay with you. But make sure that she knows and check with her social worker before the girl moves in. It can take an entire afternoon to dig and prepare a good celery trench.

CHAPTER 2

The foster home

Now we have had a preliminary glimpse at the field, shall we walk into a potential foster home and have a look around? See if it suits?

Room enough, yes, and a garden. Or any area of gravel, yard, mud, paving or unrestrained jungle serviceable as play space. At a pinch a flat within easy reach of park or open heath. Oddly enough, if you apply for registration as a daily child minder, far more stringent rules apply, such as the amount of floor and window space per child, the number of lavatories, the adequacy of safety precautions. You might think that for fostering, which is a 24-hour-a-day occupation, the overall feel of the place and overt parental pride would, at first sight, seem to suffice.

Many folk, eager to make a good impression, have a rare old clean-up in preparation for the visits of any representative of the social services. Last-minute dusting, polishing and ironing don't help at all and any attempt to join the congregation of the house-proud is a waste of time. Children, more particularly children who have hitherto not met with velvet curtains and Worcester figurines, do not often understand the differences between that which will wash and that which will spoil; that which will smash and that which will bounce back; nor that the inadvertent destruction of any given object could turn a new foster parent into one of the Furies.

Let a house, then, be primarily a home. Comfortable, both practically and atmospherically, kickable within reason, easy, and yet within the bounds of a loose order. However, a room of one's own, child-free so far as is possible, is important to most of us. I have what's known as the workroom; a tip of a place with sewing-machine, typewriter, files, books which are particularly dear or necessary, and an enormous amount of table space. Roy and Tom come in to do homework. The sick and the miserable are allowed in if proximity to me is part of the cure. Sundry welfare workers are admitted when the need for private discussion overrides the more usual open conversation concerning any child's case.

We do not all share the same standards of either veracity or respect for other people's property; thus, if we keep things like important bits of paper or items of poignant sentiment on, say, the kitchen shelf or even beneath our undies in the bedroom drawer, don't let's blame anyone besides ourselves should these irreplaceables walk. A child who has never stolen a thing in his life is rarer than the unicorn; one whose experience of being shunted about has thrown him into the deep-end of resentment is more likely than others to pay you back, innocent though you are, by nicking your prized possessions.

I present the less attractive side of fostering before recounting its more pleasurable aspects. It's only fair. For the truth is that all human beings, even very small ones, differ one from the other. The foster child is, by the nature of his position in society, inevitably burdened. He is under stress and stress itself manifests itself in many forms from the barely discernible to the heavily incomprehensible. Some shake their traumas off in a jiffy, soon settling into their second family with every outward sign of affection and contentment. Others carry their psychological wounds around year after year like a well-recognized uniform.

Most fall between; able to work through irregularities of behaviour and opinion until a plateau is reached. But not one child escapes entirely; even a relatively new infant is likely to be disturbed by a strange cot, a strange voice, a strange hand feeding him or even by a change of teat. And the more background a child gathers, the more material he is either forced to bury in his subconscious or be emotionally competent enough to come to terms with his past, his present and his unpredictable future.

Foster parents are the ones with the advantages; adult, settled, happy, with adequate material and mental resources, they must learn to come down to the level of the frightened and bewildered new child, alone in a strange land. This is not a once-and-for-all adjustment to the inner state of a young mind, but one which repeats itself in variable forms over months and years as the number of fostered children who join or pass through the family multiplies. No one standard approach suits all occasions. Indeed, a couple who may be right for one type of child could be wrong for another. Thus there are varieties even in our concept of the ideal. The patience required for good parenting, allied to love, is not the only criterion. Other qualities must be exerted according to the specific needs of each small newcomer. So our ideal must remain elastic within our overriding desire for family conformity.

One child can survive his transition only if practically ignored, allowed to inch in at his own snail's pace, given time to heal; another will trail one from room to room in desperate need of 24-hour reassurance, unable to let go lest his universe topple again.

Continuous assessment, informed by as much historical background as can be extracted from the child's social worker, becomes second nature after a while.

Let me take you into my home, whether typical or not. Though I have chosen one 24-hour stretch out of many possible examples, you will at least get some idea that fostering is a round-the-clock activity, and not without its moments of light relief.

2 a.m. Aware of rustling, turning and mild groans in next bedroom. Roy's room. He has been home for the weekend and is quite likely to have demolished his hoard of sherbet dabs, chocolate digestives and tins of Coke – part of his return luggage. Selfishly and foolishly, I ask God to make him go to sleep again. He complies, if only to teach me a lesson. Within half an hour I am woken, this time by sounds of violent throwing-up. I am there like a shot, shushing and murmuring 'never mind, darling', trying to mop up with a school shirt which has been conveniently abandoned on the floor since Friday afternoon, nipping off for a pot, a mug of water, clean sheets and blankets, newspaper for the floor and a little teddy from the nursery who has been especially requested as comforter. When I get back I find Roy throwing up all over again, though this time neatly into a plastic bag which he thoughtfully snatched from among the remains of his feast. Deathly white, he manages a weak grin through the final heavings.

Together we pile the fouled bedding on the landing, arrange pot and bathtowel handily near the bedhead, tuck in the little teddy to leeway of possible further effusions and agree, each in our separate ways, to tumble into the arms of Morpheus. It is just 3.15 a.m.

6 a.m. Alarm rings. Ben, who suffers from a chromosomal defect and who, because of attendant handicaps, is deemed worthy of the large hospital-type cot stationed in my room, struggles to a standing position and enquires brightly whether I've had a good sleep. I have not, I say tersely, and will he please lie down and waggle the bit of string which, for reasons best known to himself, has become an inseparable bedfellow.

Then I am asleep again. I do not hear teenaged Georgie get up and go to her YTS job; I do not hear the postman or the milkman and it is through a haze of disbelief that I simultaneously see and hear Hugh beside my bed. His clothing, making nonsense of the law of averages, is both inside-out and back-to-front. Would I wake up, he is very quietly saying; the telephone is ringing.

I hare downstairs barefoot, assaulted by the pile of Roy's bedding on the landling. The teacher counsellor who does not like being called the play lady is on the wire; she will visit Ben for assessment at 11.30. Yes, that will be fine: it just fits in neatly with coming home from nursery school. Horror of horrors, I see it is already 8.15. The older children must leave the house soon after half-past; the younger by ten-to-nine. Pandemonium ensues; cereals are consumed in their accustomed quantity though at a speed unrecordable by the naked eye. Roy insists that he is quite well enough for school (it is gym day) and promises to go easy on dinner. I throw on my own clothes, wrestle with Hugh's misapplied garments. Then Ben.

I tackle the changing (manual expression of both functions . . . and find out for yourselves what that entails if you're not cognizant); get him of a piece into his supportive waistcoat using screwdriver and steady hand; put on the bespoke boots and calipers. Then, miraculously to time, we (Hugh, Ben and self) set off for nursery school. On return the house will be my own for two blessed hours.

11.15 a.m. My couple of hours have been taken up almost completely by washing and coping with the sicky bedding. Carpet too. The telephone rang thrice, in each case the call being directly concerned with the children. Brian's forms have come through to the surgery; could I make an appointment for his medical? I explain that he's away at boarding school (paid for by his local authority) and that this will now have to be done by the school doctor. The speech therapist then cancelled tomorrow's slot for Ben but could take him at the same time next week. Then there was a *cri de coeur* from Hugh's mother. She'd wanted to come over next Saturday but 'they' wouldn't let her off work and the buses didn't fit in. If she came by train could I meet her? Yes, I said, but if you're not getting here till tea-time wouldn't it be easier to stay the night? Better to ask about a B.R. Weekender then; they're cheaper.

Fetch Hugh and Ben from nursery and get coffee for our teacher counsellor. Fortnightly visits are made to all handicapped pre-school children in the county, the point being to guide parents, encourage children and generally chart educational milestones. She stays at least an hour, progressing from simple jigsaws to colour-matching games, shapes, comparisons, number and texture. Can he put on his own vest? Brush his own teeth? Respond to his name if called from another room? Obey a simple request to fetch a given object? Does he know the names of his foster brothers and can he repeat those names? If you hand him a comb does he know what to do with it? A salt cellar? A duster? A pair of scissors?

12.30 p.m. We stand at the window, a time-honoured custom, to wave her goodbye; Ben throws a tantrum if we fail in this courtesy. The goose has laid an egg, so the three of us help one another to scramble it for lunch. We cheat; reconstitute dried potato, open a tin of baked beans in tomato sauce; decide against a pudding as being too stoutening

The daily quandary then bears upon me. If I put these two pre-schoolers down for a rest after we've eaten, then I can get on with things like this book, letters, gardening or painting the window frames. But if they rest now, they won't go to sleep until after seven this evening. I agree with myself that today I'll plump for my modicum of freedom. Bed now, I say, beaming and with outstretched arms and, like well-trained puppies, they beam back. Before I can mutter 'Heaven be praised' they're got their noses down under the quilts and are listening to Enid Blyton on the tape-machine. *Jinky and the Insects.*

I do not go for Enid Blyton much myself, and in time past, when I stuck to ideals and raw vegetables and never taking the telephone off the hook, as it is this afternoon, I would force my little ones to sleep on Vivaldi or on dear Dylan Thomas reading 'When I was young and easy under the apple boughs', in the certainty that this was filtering good stuff into their growing brains. But I know better now. Take them to see *Twelfth Night* or *A Midsummer Night's Dream* at five and they'll sit spellbound; but they'll still be refusing to go to Stratford at sixteen because Shakespeare is 'boring' and nobody in their form goes anyway.

Nobody other than long-term foster parents, with the possible exception of women with huge natural families, can experience the bliss of strings of consecutive moments void of that 'Mummy! Mummy!' cry. Perhaps it is pertinent to add here that I have been the recipient of 'Mummy! Mummy!' and sundry other such appellations for almost thirty years and I am not the longest-running foster mother by a fairish chalk.

At **2.00 p.m.** the health visitor calls in on passing. Yes, I assure her, everything is fine, but the boys are resting just now. She reminds me that, as Ben is getting on towards his fifth birthday, I ought to be putting in for the mobility allowance. Fed as we are by ugly stories in the press, it crosses my mind that this health visitor has taken it as gospel that the two smallest really are taking a midday nap. I suppose she knows me well enough not to harbour any darker suspicions. We smile goodbye and I start on the window frames, rubbing away six years' flaked gloss, sorely disfiguring my finger nails between no.3 sandpaper and ready splinters.

3.00 p.m. 'Mummy! Mummy!' The chorus is off. Curtains to the quietude of my own back yard. Ben can't get out of the cot on his own because of the famous support waistcoat, so I must go up and help. He also needs changing and seeing to again. Hugh has lost his shoes. We find them at the bottom of his bed; he had gone to sleep with them on, woken with them off.

39

3.30 I hear the merry whoop of the primary school pair as they hurtle themselves at gate, dog and bread-bin – in that order. 'We're starving! Really starving!' So it's Wonderloaf brown and red jam and a welcome-home homily from me about the difference between starvation and hunger. They go off giggling and dropping their gym stuff and a vocabulary book. I wipe a blob of jam off the bannister and suppose I'd better put the telephone on the hook again.

It responds at once. The dentist's receptionist reminds me that it is long past time for Ashley to have his check-up. In turn I remind her that Ashley is in youth custody and will thus have the advantage of a dentist visiting him for the immediate future. Meanwhile Mr W, the patient young man who calls in once a week to give Roy his piano and violin lessons, sets up his stand in the dining-room and Roy starts off with 'Round about the Maypole', which sounds very nice. Glancing out of the window I see Ben at the top of the stepladder I leaned against the fence after sandpapering the window frames. Considering the handicap of steel reinforced waistcoat, navvy's boots with calipers and total paralysis below the knees, I put that ascent on a par with me, say, going up the church steeple. Good old Ben. I resist the protective temptation to dash out and oversee his coming down. In the dark ages when I did my nursery training we were taught 'never to do for a child, particularly a handicapped child, what he can do for himself'.

4.00 p.m. I pay Mr W his modest £2, congratulate him on his Russian A-Level pass and send my love to his mother. Simultaneously I am assailed by a racket so unholy that I know it can only be Tom going for Hugh again. They are brothers, nine and four, and know all about sibling rivalry. Their fights are foul and brutal, real hate in the raw, and almost anything will blow Tom's fuse. I fly upstairs and separate them by the remote control of my own considerable yelling. Hugh comes to tell me of his little wounds, hoping for blood. Tom gives me a look so deadpan innocent that, for the nth time, I am afraid for him. He is a child who rarely shows emotion to adults. In the four months he has been with this family I have never seen him cry or light up or even look cagey. There are events shut in his past which have taught him to blank off, to withdraw into his not unintelligent cranium. Yet put him in a situation where he is alone with a child and he will burst out of that shell and fight or attempt, usually successfully, to manipulate.

He has gone into his bedroom now. The door is carefully closed. He will, if he follows his usual pattern, rearrange the furniture, the pictures, all his trappings. Here is a boy I would not leave alone in the house for two minutes. Not for his good, nor mine.

4.30 p.m. Set about getting high tea. They have a sandwich lunch at school so it's important that now they eat what's known as properly. Within reason I let the children select the menu. It's good for them to make choices, even small ones. Their lives have been so full of decisions being made for them; events and circumstances falling off a conveyor belt. Do this, go there, leave those, listen here. Roy wants tomatoes and ham and baked potatoes. We shall cheat with these by using the microwave, and he goes shopping for the meat, independence again, while I scrub the spuds.

5.30 p.m. Call Ben and Hugh in from the garden, wipe off the worst of the dirt and sit them down at table. Georgie's bus has just gone by so she'll be in soon. This is her second week at work and her self-esteem, hitherto nil, is positively sparkling. She too has been here for four or five months, the casualty of problems with a stepparent. Incidentally, she had no glimmer of an idea that she would achieve anything after leaving school except going on the dole. Her sights had been set no higher nor, presumably, had she received any encouragement to try her wings.

5.35 p.m. We are assembled, the plates filled, the mouths likewise. We are into a rather heavy discussion on the desirability, or not, of nuclear power, with graphic asides on the after-effects of the explosion at Chernobyl, including what Tom refers to as 'live-wired' lambs and what would happen if we ate their meat. Then as we momentarily pause to clear the dishes and distribute bananas and a large but sadly sunken Victoria sponge, a battered CV2 drives into the yard and I prepare myself for Georgie's social worker who, unlike most others, seldom gives prior warning of her visits.

I try hard to like this woman and I sense that she tries hard in the opposite direction, but the results of our efforts are not satisfactory. I cannot altogether go along with the silken voice, the lack of push, the bland acceptance of the *status quo*. The poor and needy must have a ball with her; the soft touch, the ready distributor of carpets, cookers and holidays on Grasmere. She's enough to make any Tory have a fit.

Georgie deals with it all today. She is already 16, old enough to show what she's made of, to manage without a go-between, to have her privacy honoured. I am proud of my new Georgie; proud that she did not take this lady's advice and 'sign on'.

6.15 p.m. Ben in the tub first, then Hugh. The whole bottle of shampoo is accidentally spilled, making a marvellous meringue-like surface to the water. Predictable, I suppose, but these two are not in the least disposed to sleep, thus there is a measure of cot-rocking, brmmming and infant singing to put up with. Then the remedial reading with Roy. I am sickened by the story, too graphically illustrated, of the old woman who finds a big toe in the road and takes it home in the basket of her motor-bike.

I long for the congenial goings-on of dear Janet and John.

Reading matter still, in the early stages, reflects in the main a child's own experiences. Do they no longer have picnics under weeping willows, no longer help Dad to wash his car on the front drive? No longer get invited to stay with kind Auntie Pat and Uncle Bob on their farm? According to remedial reading, today's infants witness Mum throwing a wet tea-towel at Dad as she calls him the equivalent of a lazy rat, thus asserting her right not to be landed with the washing-up, or that other gad-about Mum donning her fur-trimmed coat prior to attending the local bingo hall; or where the amiable sea-captain, never a one to do a mean act, gets rewarded by the plumber's twins, one perched on each knee, wetting his nice uniform.

Spelling test tomorrow. Tom joins us for a run through the list: weather, clouds, rain, blizzard, shower, thermometer and meteorology. This leads on to gathering the swimming gear for school, cleaning the shoes, searching for shirts and putting the lunches into little plastic boxes.

7.30 p.m. Tom's father telephones and I have a quick and reassuring word and then call the child down. I learn that both mother and father will be visiting next Thursday. Father will bring his tools and mend the bicycle. Good.

8.00 p.m. Boys to bed. Let them read as long as they like and put their own lights out. I get in the fourth load of washing since morning. Let Georgie off the ironing because it's her day-release for Tech. tomorrow and she's got reading to do. Just iron the shirts; fold the rest up; clear the general debris of the day; shut the fowls up; feed cats and dog; cover guinea pig and rabbit against chill night air; write postcards to Brian at school and Ashley (no need to repeat where he is) and a grown-up letter to James at his barracks.

9.00 p.m. Yes, goodnight, Georgie. Sensible of you to get to bed early. I'll probably do the same. God bless.

Some days there are hospital appointments, school meetings, open days, speech therapy, Cubs, karate, concerts, plays, birthday parties, six-monthly reviews (compulsory), visiting physio (Ben) or visits from any of the other various workers currently involved with 'my' children.

Fostering then, even if you limit yourself to one at a time, is tantamount to a sort of holistic erosion (mind, body and spirit). It can also become addictive; once you prove buoyant enough to keep afloat you just keep on. And on.

CHAPTER 3

Suited to fostering?

Now that you have some idea of what fostering is about, how do you think *you* would shape up? In which of the many categories of foster parent do you see yourself? Are you a partner in a stable happy marriage? If so, you may count as ideal. Ideally, of course, the ideal foster parent should be married to another such ideal. And very often she is. I speak of 'she' unguardedly because, in spite of all the role reversal and flattening of theoretical gender differences, it is almost always the female who looks after the child. Exceptions to this generalization please make allowances; and forgive me.

Girls, women, ladies even, nature's mothers, are more able to give unconditional love to a child in passing; men less so. Yet a male, attached to such an open-hearted female and also head-over-heels for family life, makes a good foster father. But don't think it ends there; love, family piety and good intentions are not enough.

But today, where the ideal has been redefined more broadly as an ability to pick up any strange child and instinctively know what's good for him, the classification of an ideal parent is undergoing a sea-change. Whereas, years ago, foster father and mother were invariably legally joined, and the single woman who took in children was something of a sore thumb, we now see almost every combination of domestic relationship claiming a right to foster; the catchment area is broadening. Whether we agree with the current vogue of freedom for every individual, regardless of mental, physical or moral calibre, to experience copulation, pregnancy, birth and the long haul of parenthood is by the way. What is absolutely certain is that members of most minority groups should be able, with approval, to make an application to foster. And that application must be given the same initial consideration as any more conventional one.

Many of the deviations from our ideal will stand no more than a hair's-breadth chance. Overt transvestites, for instance, are notoriously difficult to fit into any family which includes the coming and going of children. I recall with concern the teenaged twins who shared this roof for a while. These girls' naval officer father had rung the changes between shot-silk evening gowns, denim boiler suits and the full and splendid rig of a Lieutenant-Commander. They were confused girls, torn between ... I was going to say ... the devil and the deep blue sea.

Homosexual couples with steady relationships are beginning to feature on social services lists of approved foster parents; and, oddly enough, more male couples take on fostering than female couples. This could mean that women partners are less able to break out of the intensity of their commitment to each other into the magnanimity of building and sharing.

Extra care, over and above the norm, must be taken when selecting children for any of the more unusual placements on offer. Few, if any, children up to the age of puberty can fully understand adult emotions. That 'Daddy loves Mummy' is as acceptable as 'Daddy and Mummy love me' is taken for granted. This comfortable assurance is devoid of any conscious sexuality. To expect a normally developing child to come to terms with the concept of two parents being of the same gender is unreasonable. This is my opinion; it need not be yours.

Short-stay or school-holidays fostering which is of a predictable duration, where there is no question of a real parent image resulting, can provide a valuable trial period in households not previously seen as 'normal'. However, children over about seven who are beyond innocent and uncritical acceptance of unusual situations are liable to be subjected to the slings and arrows of contemporaries and may find themselves picked on and teased. It takes a child of strong character to withstand the pressure, so it is hardly fair to place him with a gay couple.

Parenting in the true sense, based on the degree of love and commitment necessary for the setting up of a real family, maybe for life, can be undertaken on a more testing level. Children with Down's Syndrome or similarly handicapped or the out-and-out misfits are by the nature of their difference on the whole incapable of criticizing. They both receive and offer love unequivocally, are above or beyond being hurt by the thoughtless opinions of others and are more able than many to appreciate a good home when they find it.

The ideal for this category of substitute parents consists of a kindly and sympathetic couple who have created, over a number of faithful years, a happy establishment. They are not camp. They do not cause their neighbours to raise an eyebrow. They are an honest, affectionate pair who possess heart enough to take a child in their single-sex family. Socially they mix easily and are not necessarily viewed by friends and acquaintances as gay, but as human beings in their own right. If they are realistic when they make an application to foster, they will see that at least one of their referees is 'straight'.

Single foster fathers have cropped up in both fact and fiction over long years. Kindly, self-giving Silas Marner and, in more recent times, the television series in which the house was too tidy, too dotted with valuables, too easily-run for words called 'Only Uncle'. Even so, the local authorities still view unattached males in the role of carers with some trepidation.

Social services departments step extremely cautiously; they are afraid of the man's motives, his sexual proclivities, and, frankly, his ability to cope with the everyday care of someone else's child. It's a cleft stick for them. If they dismiss the application out of hand simply because the man's a man, they are leaning against the Sexual Discrimination Act, yet, if they bend over backwards to comply with the equal status dogma, they might be worried by the risk they would be taking, for any adverse consequences would rebound onto their shoulders.

Point number one: all single men are not homosexual any more than all single women are. Point number two: whereas it is joyously accepted that a single mother can fall into the ideal bracket and become a valued part of the fostering team, the male aspirant is less readily seized upon by the social services departments, despite the fact that they are without exception always desperate for additional fostering places.

There are, granted, countless men bringing up families single-handed; men who are widowed or otherwise left holding the baby. Some are dedicated enough to fly in the face of neighbours' opinions and give up work in order to do their damnedest to rear normal, healthy, emotionally uncomplicated children. My friend Graham, for instance, has brought up four with a confident aplomb which would put many a woman-dominated home to shame, though with what social/mental sacrifice to himself I refrain from describing. The existence of fortuitous situations such as these is frequently used in argument and as justification by unattached men who want to foster. But it is no just comparison. The child you already know, who is part of your flesh and who most likely shares your loss, grief or anger, cannot be seen in the same context as any extraneous child being grafted on through officially supervised channels.

There is also the question of finance. Fostering brings a weekly (or fortnightly, according to your council's habits) maintenance cheque, in arrears. With the exception of severely disabled or excruciatingly badly behaved children, there is no wage for fosterers. Any monetary incentive to take on a difficult child is considered to be a reward element by HM Inspector of Taxes, and treated as income. For any aspiring male foster parent, at best able to keep his job between school hours and allowing for measles, this restriction could reduce the household's standard of living at a rate of knots. For nine-tenths of the population remain of the opinion that men, even though they be full-time fathers, should still go out to work. The full-time mother, a description which also includes the woman without progeny of her own but with fostered children, does not suffer from this conventional attitude. It may be wrong, unfair, even against social practicalities, but it is so. Any foster father who opts for help from the DHSS should be prepared to cope with the neighbours' brickbats as well as their congratulations.

Unattached women present a much safer proposition for the beleaguered social services. Less of an over-all risk, less of a public question-mark, they conform, even at application stage, to an acceptable parenting image. So, let us concede that our chances, merely by being female, are weighted favourably from the start.

For myself, now almost at the end of my third decade of fostering, I peer back into my mid-twenties when it all began. With two of my four children already in the cradle and my marriage intact, I was perhaps considered to be ready-made, within the ideal group. Being accepted for registration must then have been so painless that I cannot now recall any single part of that vetting. I imagine that my earlier training both in nursery nursing and midwifery must have helped me on my way.

After my marriage evaporated, after, too, a tiny pause for readjustment during which I had quite enough to do with five children, four of my own loins and the first of the adopted ones, I recovered my scattered faculties, learned to cope with a new and decision-laden life, and ploughed for all I was worth into fostering.

I timed my entrance onto the single-parent platform well; it was the middle of the Swinging Sixties, when marriage breakdown became a commonplace statistic. The unmarried mother, too, was beginning to get a new image. No longer was she thought, according to sentiment, fast, brazen, unlucky, caught out or unfortunate. Neither were she and her baby, however and by whomsoever begotten, pressured by social attitudes into separation. Now, buoyed up by the state and/or maintenance from ex-spouses or putative fathers, women bringing up children on their own took their place in society and got on with the job very nicely, thank you.

The single foster mother began to show her worth concurrently with the emergence of the fatherless-by-choice family and its coincidence with the general trend of cutting down, or even abolishing, institutional places in favour of boarding out. Economic grounds and therapeutic values each played a part.

As Ruth, an unmarried woman who has taken into her home over a dozen children within the last decade, says, 'any person may think she doesn't fit into the traditional "parenting" slot. All I can say is this, how many of us live in traditional homes anyway? The final conclusion must be that is better to be loved by someone than to spend your childhood in an emotional wilderness. Just who that someone is isn't all that relevant. It's not even necessary to act as a Mummy or a Daddy. Just someone to be there, to be interested, loving, reliable. Colour, creed, sex, who minds? That's all unimportant so long as someone cares for you.'

Then there are considerations of age; is one group more or less successful than another? On the whole, there is an obligation to match the parents' age with that of the given child's own years. Surrogacy should be able to pass for real parenthood in a crowd. Still, it isn't much good separating the fact of age from all the other essential qualities; everything has to come together in order to achieve paragon status, though it doesn't often turn out that way.

The vast majority of fosterers fall between the middle twenties and middle forties. Sitting ducks, they are caught at home with their own growing families. Their prime function is still as parents and the scene is set. All equipment, in the form of nursery furniture and so on, is still in the house, even if gathering dust in the loft. The urge to move over and make room needs no more of a nudge than an appealing notice in a local paper. That is, if all else fits the bill.

Some foster parents, more particularly those living within the hard-pressed London boroughs, are swinging into the job as early as nineteen or twenty. (Remember, a nursery nurse can be qualified at eighteen.) Most of these very young foster mothers are registerd for taking babies, say under three, which fits in with the situational matching of ages. Thus Donna, a girl working with one of the south London boroughs and herself the mother of a small son, specializes in infants under one year old and finds this works particularly well. Living in a flat with no space for a play area, she would find life with more than one active toddler difficult. Her area office understands her problem and, though Donna is fully qualified in child care for children of all ages, only offers her the very young, and all her children are placed on a short-term basis.

In the natural course of events we see foster parents of forty-plus beginning to slacken off as their own children and long-stay fostered children leave school and go out into the world. Having given, yes, it is a gift, a couple of decades or so to the nurturing of their own and other people's offspring, they've had enough. They want now to have some time to be together, to do their own thing, to throw off weighty ties and slow the pace. All they have to do is to say so; freedom is just a telephone call away.

However, for a minority of stalwarts fostering takes over; becomes the be-all and end-all; develops into an unalterable way of life. Even though former children have in their turn become mothers and fathers, the basic nursery routine within the old home welcomes new generations. The fosterers become stuck in an agreeable state of arrested development, one stage on from Peter Pan, indefinitely trapped in parenthood. Generally this perpetual motion is brought about almost inadvertently by the chance overlap of placements. Busy with, say, a couple of youngsters just into secondary school and offered, say, a child at the top end of primary school, the elastic-sided foster parent grafts on another member of the family while, at the same time, guaranteeing herself another eighteen months' toil in the rearing pen. This could, and does, almost unwittingly, make for a lifetime's work.

Bear in mind, too, that often a child who is received for just a few weeks while a permanent placement is found will remain part of the domestic circus for years. Over the past twelve months alone I have taken on three new children and am thus, in my dotage, the proxy mother of another four-year-old, his brother aged ten and yet another separate girl who just came for a weekend. None of these recent additions, though now loved and very much part of us, falls under the heading of planned parenthood.

Many older couples, single women and a few unusual men, who look upon fostering as far more than a sideline to their lives, extend this kindergarten regime into their sixties and seventies, sallying forth like St Elizabeth, mother of John the Baptist, with perambulators, filling their bathrooms with disposable nappies and their sitting rooms with Lego. Yet there is, to my knowledge, no evidence to support the theory that children who receive care and affection from these long-stayers are disadvantaged by the double generation gap.

I'm not suggesting that children living with older foster parents remain blissfully unaware of the chasm. After all, they observe nippy young mothers and cricket-playing fathers and mingle with the comparatively sprightly relatives of their classmates, and so on. My own children have often been known to lag behind, or walk briskly in front, when out and about for all the world to see. James has many a time and oft suggested that I dye my faded locks a more brilliant hue and once, not so long ago, I was handed the dubious compliment, 'Mummy, d'you know you look quite young if you don't turn round?'

I am touched by requests for stories of the olden days when I was a girl in the 1940s. At the school gate, where parents of all ages are at their most vulnerable and therefore where I would expect derision against the aged parent to be more marked, I am greeted happily and with gusto by all who call my shabby house home.

It wasn't so long ago that a grandmother bringing up her illegitimate grandchild was seen as commonplace. Moreover, before the relatively recent advent of reliable contraceptives, it was not all that unusual for women up to the age of fifty to be delivered of their final infant. So this form of elderly mothering is hardly new.

However, the present breed of teenager is, by virtue of social and historical change, brand new. Our antediluvian environment and old-fashioned insistence on, say, decent manners at table, could be found irksome. Or plain amusing. You'd never guess how many cannot so much as wield the tools; all nourishment having hitherto been conveyed to the mouth by means of slapping it into a slice of bread, producing a sort of instant pasty, and hemming the sides down with the fingers. Mashed potato and gravy, fried eggs and chips, beef mince and peas; heap the lot into slabs of Wonderloaf and go at it like a being recently reclaimed from the wild.

Likewise the matter of speech. We, the supposed ideals of the old school, may abhor the poverty of language and grossness of four-letter words which can arrive with a new child. We know for certain that this oral handicap will spread like impetigo through the settled children if we turn a deaf ear. Thus we make it clear from day one that swearing isn't on. We do not stand cheek. We do not allow ourselves to be bossed or manipulated by verbal wiles.

If the placement seems likely to become a protracted one we may soon begin to correct, diplomatically, the double negatives, the shipwrecked aitches, the request to 'shove dahn the bu'er then'. On the other hand, or out of the other side of the mouth if you like, consideration must always be given to the child's background and the one to which he may be required to return. He has his loyalties. There must be no hint of mockery, no implied criticism of the norm he has acquired within his own family. Pitfalls are not all that easy to avoid.

Take Georgie for example. Invited home for the first time after being here with us for six months, she was delighted to see her mother and little sisters again, though repelled as before by her inebriate stepfather. But she was thrown by the situation because she couldn't easily understand what they were saying. Such is the gently invasive osmosis occasioned by proximity; one set of habits imperceptibly exchanged for another. The child is almost infinitely malleable. 'Aren't we good enough for you any more, then?' sneered the awful stepfather. 'No,' replied Georgie, 'at any rate *you're* not.'

It is more often the teenagers, not the little ones, who come unstuck. A hefty generation gap, if encountered by a young person full of rebellion, frustration and, incongruously, a sort of pseudo-worldliness, is often strewn with methaphorical mines. We, the fuddy-duddies, are well into the 'old dogs and new spots' syndrome. Mohican hairdo's and fixing gel, personal radios spilling out the thump of a primeval heartbeat, the refusal to eat anything but limp tape from a plastic snack pot, the mumbled sarcasm from an immature anarchist – any of these could easily prove too much for a comfortable and homely woman past her prime. Yet, perversely, over and over again one finds local authorities anxious to foster older children in a vain attempt to 'match' the older foster parent. Wealth of experience and know-how may be supposed to prepare one for all-comers, but in reality it is the tear-aways, the mods, the physically sophisticated and sexually proficient who make us feel like beings from a bygone age. Of course there are exceptions, there always are, like Mabel English of Liverpool who was still taking in recalcitrant teenagers at an age when most of her contemporaries would be cosy as robins in a twilight home.

'When I was fourteen . . .' I could well think, when coming to mental grips with a pregnant third-former or a well-proportioned madam with her neck decorated by three studded dog collars and a livid love-bite, . . . 'when I was fourteen I was still in bottle-green knickers.' So what?

Foster homes are to be found in all parts of the country; in urban, suburban and rural areas. It might therefore be supposed that any single child unfortunate enough to need care in the official sense would stand a highish chance of being transferred to a background broadly similar to his own. Similar, that is, in social and cultural terms; not, obviously, in habits and norms of behaviour. Yet that is not always so; not at all. Both geography and supply and demand make their own variants.

Take the towns and cities. Accepted norms prevail more frequently here, where departments are dealing with greater numbers and have greater choice; and where common social landmarks and occasions make for an integrated community. Schools, churches, clubs and organizations; shopping centres, cinemas and parks – these are the statics in an urban placement and can create a cradle of reassurance for a child dispossessed of the humans he knows. More blue-collar families from built-up areas opt for fostering, perhaps because unemployment leads to two parents being at home all day who are better able to make a good job of it than one.

Out in the suburbs, with inroads of gentrification, the fostering scene spans a wider social band. Here the traditional hearts of gold find themselves joined by the equally benevolent trendies with both a social conscience and a belief in the joy of parenthood. They are also to be found in fair numbers in university cities. These placements are lovely for the long-stay foster child placed young. Lots of stimulation, consideration, widening of horizons and coming to terms with the infant self. Yet it can be confusing and even shocking for the child on the run from a social blackspot or tagged with the label of slow, shy, or rejected. The overt love, earnest caring and litmus-like understanding to be expected from sharp and perspicacious minds are marvellous but the brilliance of their machinery must be tempered, must be introduced gradually to an invading child lest he become crushed by his own mantle of inadequacy and inferiority.

Now to the little towns, the villages, the Styx: away from the boroughs where the social workers, themselves often in short supply and sometimes sorely short on training, attempt to cope with two or three times the recommended case-load. In the countryside the pressure eases and the pace slows. The fostered child can, after the traumatic period of settling in, dip his toes in what amounts to healing waters. He can, but the metamorphosis is not inevitable. Here, given that all else is well, he may be a true boy, feel the weather and test the soft ground under his wellies; he may play in the ditches until he's soaked and filthy; watch the stars from an open field; see the cows calve, the controversial hunt ride by, the badgers cross the road ponderously within the beam of a car's headlights.

But even with this wide spectrum of choice, the real dilemma remains. The vast majority of children taken into council care, for whatever reason, save perhaps that of physical or mental handicap, come from backgrounds where motivated intellect and ambition are not seen as priorities. Sometimes the illness of one or both parents overrides the possibility of adequate caring and sometimes there is total relinquishment of responsibility. All the reasons for being taken into care stem, in the main, from these points, and, with obvious exceptions of real hardship, ill-health and social confusion, these under-eighteen casualties of society are drawn from the great and ever-multiplying British sub-culture.

As Major remarked so succinctly in Orwell's *Animal Farm*, 'all animals are equal, but some are more equal than others'. It is just that random uncertainty of lifestyle and stability endured by the others which feeds the system. The framework of domestic cohesion has fragmented; the human being's rights are upheld against any modicum of common sense; our education system hails the mediocre as a satisfactory summit. What hope is there for children born at the bottom of the pile?

Those more fortunate, lucky, tenacious or dogged enough to acquire knowledge, conscious happiness and financial security, smart enough to know when to stop or when to seek help out of the public eye, these privileged persons seldom come to the professional notice of social services. Thus it is rare for them to fall within the scope of fostering. Any exceptions to this class – OK, you try to find another word for it – this class filtering must involve the care or schooling predominantly of severely handi-capped or disturbed children for whom the alternative of remaining at home is impracticable or non-effective.

Right through the spectrum, from the normal placement requiring no more than common or garden parental hand-ling to the family deliberately selected for its specialized skills, essential if the given child is to progress or even hold his own, one finds that two-thirds of foster families are generally professionals and semi-professionals. School teachers, university lecturers, academics and people connected with the arts in general; clergymen of all dyes, farmers, builders and taxi drivers – all feature. So do the thoroughly settled and comfortable families within the unskilled bracket.

The yuppies do not foster, nor do the young fogies, nor father-dominated families, nor materialists. The unemployed do, the retired do, the free-and-easies do, the unassumingly benevolent do.

I have yet to meet a social worker who concurrently fosters a child.

CHAPTER 4

Facts of fostering: the extended lifestyle

Over 40,000 families throughout the United Kingdom are involved in fostering. Some stick out as such by sheer strength of number; others settle down discreetly, wedging themselves in between ordinary families so that nobody would know the difference. Most, us included, hang in the middle, unusual in our presentation of human ebb and flow, drawing attention by this diversity of family members and the adventures befalling them: child in hospital for rotation of left foot, child set the house on fire, child missing all night and found by police in airing cupboard, child won scholarship to public school, child cautioned on account of shoplifting, writing dubious graffiti, throwing bicycle through plate glass window.

The milk bottles delivered to our steps may resemble the serried ranks of the Light Brigade. Twenty loaves of bread a week count as nothing. Neighbours leave bunches of rhubarb at the back door, or gooseberries, or carrier-bags of outgrown but not worn-out clothes. Village maidens, and in our case dear Tony, village lad, turn up after tea to help bath the babies or test the school spellings or clean the seven pairs of shoes for tomorrow.

The back kitchen is strewn with wellingtons. The hooks behind the doors are overburdened with haphazard overcoats, anoraks, snowsuits. The mug in the bathroom wears its toothbrushes as a vase might display chrysanthemums. Not only does washing dangle from the outdoor line but from the strings threaded east to west across the kitchen, over a cord in the greenhouse and heaped round the hot tank in the airing cupboard. The washing machine's hum is permanent background noise; so, on crisis days, is the telephone bell.

These are but samples of the externals, but the mind and energy too take on a recognizably fostering slant. Like the parents of a newborn babe, our ears are constantly pricked for sound. At night we wake at a pin's drop. We home in on toothache or tummy upset or a bout of homesickness almost before the sufferer himself has registered the discomfort. We learn, over years, to be one ahead; averting quarrels, diverting trouble, prompting, reminding and insisting; dinner money? gym shorts? thank-you letters?

Our body-clock becomes more amenable to unpremeditated shift-work. Some nights we are up till two patching trousers; woken at five by a child who thinks he's heard a bogeyman tapping, like Heathcliff at his third-floor window; bothered by the alarm at six-thirty; then by Little Goody Twoshoes bearing a revolting, cold, grey cup of tea at seven. The next evening a dead calm will tempt one to bed at ten and the night will last till eight in the morning – deep, solid peace.

Having weathered the first hectic years, a really entrenched foster family tends to forget what easy domestic life is like. The four-square view of mother, father, home and 'own' children, from the other side of the fence, fluctuates between green envy on bad days to giddy thankfulness on the best of days, for our extraordinary manner of carrying on. No two days are the same; there is never any certainty as to how many little heads, not infrequently lousy, will rest upon our pillows tonight; there is never the complacency of knowing that all problems are solved, all corners rounded.

For myself, I really admire any man, in particular the working man beavering all day in the rates department of county hall or in the chicken factory or in the gents' outfitting at the Co-op, any man who can give up his lovely evenings and weekends, ad infinitum, to other people's children. I am bound to say, whatever the modern opinion to the contrary, that women are on the whole more willing to offer parenthood to extraneous young. In fact, if the decision to foster rested wholly with the woman and vetting for approval relied less on the whole circus, then the 45,000 children in this country who are today in line for substitute homes would be taken up like doves to the cote.

Of course it's ridiculous, nowadays, to consider the mother as being anything but part (and still the most important) of the package. Assiduous concern is paid, in planning, to the family as a spread. If the whole family does not present a unanimous front in favour of taking on a spare child or two, then its suitability for doing so must officially be seen as doubtful.

Foster families are to be found throughout the country. We are part of the community, part of the social services and financially buoyed up by local government funds. In the present climate of 'integration or bust' our services are jealously sought, each area office keeping us to themselves in so far as they can. The annual Foster Care Week takes place in the first week in May and aims at recruitment and pushing information, yet receives a poor response from an otherwise open-handed public. The Englishman's home is his castle, and it is private to boot. He does not rush to open his front door to miscellaneous children; he does not relish involvement with their close relatives, many of whom strive to follow their children's lives in more ways than just the accepted visiting, whether through affection, curiosity or a terrible desperation.

Being a neighbour to a fostering family can be quite interesting, so I'm told; it is sometimes like having one's own soap opera on the spot. It also offers an opportunity to show munificence without shouldering responsibility, rather like being a grandparent. Our own neighbours sometimes take a cross-section of the children out to a fête or a steam rally or a motorbike scramble. It relieves me of the rougher edges of the burden for a few hours, is enormously appreciated, and is especially interesting if it elicits a fresh view on a child. X, I'm assured, is an absolute angel. Y, is, frankly, a pig. Z needs therapy for his masochistic tendencies.

Neighbours' telephone numbers are essential. There are times when you are stuck in the hospital waiting-room, ready to take your turn for Ben's X-rays or Roy's hearing test, while the others are due to come out of school ten miles away. Ring the changes; do not ask the same people to do duty too often. And thank them with a box of chocolates when you do.

Another unusual, and perhaps for these days, extra-ordinary feature of many a foster family is the standard of manners to be found therein. I can say, unblushingly, how often kindly folk tell me how polite and well spoken my children are, and I am not alone in this. Exceptions there are, naturally, but not many. In these days of yobdom, discourtesy and shucks-to-you, it is perhaps a reversal of the current trend. Foster children, who already carry the stigma of being in care, must be helped to be as good as and, if possible, better than their peers. Few will, in fact, make the professions; most will find middle-of-the-road employment in the future; some will find it a full-time job even to keep their heads above the incoming tides. Yet if they present themselves well they could perhaps put an edge on the more settled, brainier, parent-backed youngster who sprawls like a squid on a fishmonger's slab, doesn't look an interviewer in the eye and has a vocabulary largely consisting of 'yaaah' and 'naaah'.

I have noticed that one or two of my relatives do not make much of my grafted family. There has been mention of their rates being used to fund oats for our porridge and powder for our indefatigable Zanussi. They have commented on those who dribble and stare, those who scratch without inhibition or who occasionally wear a wet stain on the trousers. People under our system of government are free to make up their own minds about the ramifications of our welfare system and the points awarded for the appearance of any recipient of that system's funding. We learn to take it; to stand up for our family calmly; to make our points without raising blood pressure.

My closest dears, all my grown-up children, have always been intimately concerned with the world of fostering. They are the real aunts and uncles; the under-standers of uncertain behaviour, of wet beds, of new-comers withdrawn or with few talents. I love them for it. It is they who are generous at birthdays and Christmas, they who stand up, even sometimes against me, for the child who goes his own way regardless of my bossy guidance. They never fail with their tender loving care.

Friends accept our lifestyle as they accept us. The children, the hub of this house, interest them, just as their children interest us. We sometimes join in together for outings, meals, walks, picnics; we talk out our worries and fears together and help each other to sort out our problems. Friends are valuable and I lean on them. Sometimes we even swap children for a day, a weekend, part of a half-term holiday. Then there are other foster families, met through the NFCA or at similar get-togethers, who feature high on my list of intimates as do the parents of some of 'my' children.

Friends seem to be able to take a more relaxed, more objective view of the strangers in our midst than do our own relations. Some just see it as my job, as sometimes I do too, particularly when caring for short-term visitors who are full-throated hyperactive insomniacs. Some see it as a fixation, or a cause, or a Freudian refusal to admit to increasing years, or, the hardest to accept, a need to be needed. But the one constant is their sympathy, if not always understanding. I value my friends for their listening ears, their advice, their affection and their concern for the children.

We ought to feel proud, for we, with our muddled airing-cupboards, our missed appointments, our worn carpets and kicked bannisters, are considered to be better for the children than any institution in the land. As fosterers our homes are considered desirable shelter for immature human beings however distressed they are.

Considered by whom? The child-care boffins, the theorists, the workers in the fields. All but the most hard-boiled of these people who have the best interests of the child at heart vote for home with a small h, where an ordinary child will find a warm atmosphere, a pleasant combination of freedom and personal security, the right to retain his individuality and, most, to matter as a growing person in the eyes of a parent-figure to whom he belongs. Actually nearly half of all children in care are with foster families; all, indeed, for whom foster homes are forthcoming.

Based on this premise, the small family placement is right, in theory, for every type of child from nought to eighteen. It is certainly a fact that even some of the most severely handicapped children are currently fostered successfully whereas ten years ago they would have been faced with a lifetime in institutional care. Thus it is that many children, formerly predestined to a life void of true family, can now look forward to a meaningful existence. In many ways it is a good thing that Homes and residential establishments are being phased out in some areas, drastically reduced in others.

In a perfect world all children would have a home, their own loving parents, fun and privacy; in a perfect world all children, however unfortunate, would be amenable and lovely.

But we do not live in a perfect world. There are children of all ages from infancy to late teens who by any yardstick are difficult to live with 24 hours a day. I do not apportion blame or try to explain such deviancy but I do know, for I have met, sheltered and been exhausted by them, that there are children who don't fit into other people's homes any more than they fitted into their own.

The persistent destroyers, the brigade who trust nobody, the sadistic, including the out-and-out bully, the chronic kickers against parents and parent-figures; few if any of these children find themselves able to settle with equanimity into an affectionate family setting. I don't say that they would never be able to integrate into a tight-knit household, but there is a period when it is actually bad policy to wish these tearaways on to an emotionally secure family group.

A spell in a residential establishment (Home with a capital H), whether for a few weeks, months or even years, can stabilize a child by removing him from the obligation to relate to one or more parent-figure. He can get to know himself, he can learn to integrate with his peers while also being free to regard staff as paid employees rather than surrogates. He may be able to escape from the past shackles of a family which, for one or many reasons, did not fit him. He may find it easier too to accept guidance from those who are not, or who are not striving to become, parents.

Another type of child who could well be grateful for not having to attempt to integrate with a substitute family is the one who is weathering the iron grief of losing his own biological father and/or mother. Death, divorce, separation, abandonment; all can produce a sense of loss of such devastation that it cannot be papered over by understudies of any kind or even any kindness. 'Keep off' is the message sent out by this crumpled child, 'leave me to come back in my own time. Don't make me say I'm fond of you. I want my real mother. My real father.'

So, although fostering and foster families are seen as preferable to an institution, where marvellous father-figures

and mother-figures, warmth and cosiness and a room of
one's own are to be found, we ought not necessarily to be
seen automatically as first choice.

The closing of Homes has not kept pace with the
recruitment of foster parents. The shortages of places and
parents are pretty well country-wide. We are faced with
the anomaly of there being children in Homes waiting
for suitable foster parents while, simultaneously, there
are a number of almost scandalously unsuitable children
disrupting the tranquillity of foster families when they
would be better in residential care.

The actual running of a foster home creates a certain
strain. If anyone tries to tell you that such a circus can be
equated with a large Victorian family or resembles a small
children's home they are ignorant of the practical facts.
The structure of a fostered family is often by its nature
uneven. Not only is the age-range dissimilar from that of
a normal familial gestation, there being perhaps several
groups of same-age children and large gaps: there is also
considerable divergency between the length of time that
any of these children may be with you. Currently, for
instance, I have, among others, two boys aged eleven and
three aged six. One of the former has been with us since
he was two, the other came in as an emergency for a few
weeks a couple of years ago. The pecking order, in such
cases, gets awry.

The 'senior' 11-year-old happens to be a bit of a tender
plant; his little heart is soft as moss, his tears are worn
near the surface; he doesn't know what motivation is. Into
his life came this temporary contemporary; a rumbustious
know-all, unsquashable, superior as kings. This new boy
could run faster than the dog; could jump from the
15-foot yard wall; knew grown-up secrets and used every
four-letter word known to the underworld.

The place of the original child was in his own eyes
shifted. He was, if only temporarily, pitted against a

self-styled demigod. Tough. Worse, the few weeks came and went and one year, and then two, turned full circle. Emergency short term slid into long term; the limited period of showing a stiff upper lip in the face of a more gifted opponent turned into a full-time and permanent battle for place.

Foster parents frequently have to umpire such confrontations of unequals. The gentler strengths of the physically and mentally weaker child have to be pointed out tactfully while the forcefulness of the other must be tempered.

This is but one example of the kinds of differences, both in situation and management, between a family with its own carefully spaced children and one where they are introduced sporadically through the medium of the welfare services. Each individual, of whatever temperament, must be protected and respected within the cohesive whole of private family life; it is not always easy to do so.

A large foster family also differs from the ordinary household in its budgeting requirements. More time has to be spent over planning and going a-marketing; the shopping list may fill an entire page of an exercise book. There are certain preferences to be acknowledged; rusks and Ostermilk may turn up on the list over decades, as though some everlasting baby refuses to grow up; great bales of nappies are always on it and so, it seems, are cereals in almost limitless quantities.

We stagger about with this never-decreasing burden of consumer goods. Different children assist on each sortie, selecting favourites, insisting upon oven chips or mauve toilet paper or spaghetti shaped like the Loch Ness Monster, crying for the lavatory in the middle of Tesco, leaving an odd shoe in the car park.

Then too, some children, it has to be admitted, more especially those whom we have not yet trained up into little ladies and gentlemen, tend to let their fingers lead them astray while out shopping. Some, it must be said in their favour, do not know it is wrong. Indeed, some have actually been instructed to exercise such old tricks. Take, if you can, a corner shop in the old tradition; wander round and select with your eye any useful item which is out of reach. While kind but antiquated shopkeeper is stretching up to knock down the topmost Shredded Wheat, child-trainee must nip like a squib to pocket cigarettes, half a pound of butter, a slab of cheese or any other worthwhile and handily-sized commodity. Another trick learned while young is, in tandem with an adult or older sibling, to pocket the goods while that companion and almost every other human being in the shop is gathering up the scattered small change which has been deliberately dropped.

Dear foster parents, keep your line of vision clear and attempt to remain at least one jump ahead of any newcomers who may once have been Fagin's children. Others, of course, innocent of former training, will start on a thieving career after having been placed with you in order to draw attention to unfairness, anger, moroseness, real unhappiness. A child in this unprofessional shop-lifting category could be saying that he hates the social worker, his parents, the welfare, you, the world. Try to dissipate this hate; give him your time; let him talk if he will; make every effort to tease out the bitterness. Encourage him, by any means possible, to make redress; send the stuff back; send or take the money for it; write a note; go and say sorry. Let the end of the affair match the guts or the frailty of the child.

Mammoth purchasing does not only pertain to groceries and baby gear. Lavish spending is also required on the peripherals of living. There are the giant E3s of detergents, the litres of washing-up liquid, the packs of 36-at-a-time loo paper; bubble bath, shampoo (including nit shampoo),

Vim and general scourers galore. We use half a dozen Hoover bags where other families use one; wear out the ball-bearings of washing machines; suffer burned-out pans and smashed crockery well in excess of the average. We too wear out quicker. Avoid the precious or the hard-to-replace; avoid the cheap and unreliable; go for maximum durability.

It costs, then, to run a foster family even half efficiently. So we come to the maintenance payments, that manna from the finance department of county hall which, in theory, covers most expenses incurred, absorbed or defrayed by children large and small. Some areas pay by the fortnight, most by the week, all always in arrears. Each has its own rates of payment since there is no statutory standard allowance for fostered children. Toiling proxies in, say, Powys and Suffolk may be in receipt of less than three-quarters of the payment received by foster parents in the more generous Midland counties. The London boroughs in general pay the most but, even taking into account higher costs of living, the differences between districts are enormous, particularly when considering the short-term allowances, which can be as much as double the long-term.

The National Foster Care Association, the voice of both fosterer and fostered, sets down a recommended scale of allowances which are reviewed each year. This scale is increasingly being heeded by councils throughout Britain, though it is not mandatory. In most areas, the cheque can be said to be adequate, in some positively munificent. The scale slides upwards with age and often looks like riches in comparison with the relatively stingy Child Benefit drawn by everyday parents for their own offspring. Government benefits are after all not intended to cover all needs of a child within his family. Many of these are met by the breadwinner's earnings or allowances, including Family Income Supplement.

Foster families come from all walks of life. Some from the top 10% can afford to regard the county allowances as cream on the milk; others couldn't even consider taking a child, let alone two, unless every last groat of outlay was recompensed. Again, most of us lie between these two poles; glad for the sound of the manilla envelope as it falls on the mat, dependent upon it for basics, yet not going spare in the odd week when the whole lot is swallowed up on a pair of decent fell-boots. One does not, somehow, bleat about each penny spent unless one is genuinely in straitened circumstances.

Regular extra expenses are always eligible for payment, and are, in my experience, almost always met. The endless mileage to and from parents, to hospital and clinic, to swimming pool and sports clubs, to Cubs and Brownies: all may be claimed. Holidays too are covered in almost every particular, some areas making a lump sum but on request only; others making a lump sum willy-nilly; some increasing the regular allowance throughout the year so that money can be saved for the summer beano.

To my mind the middle way is best. The holiday cash does make an impression on the budget; it arrives at the start of what we take to be the warm weather, just when the ice-cream van is beginning to chime Handel's 'Largo' round the estates, when day trips from school proliferate and the sunshine tempts us to pack up and go forth into the expensive outdoors. The holiday at home, stretched over weeks with treat after treat, can work out to be as costly as seven days in Yarmouth.

You are given initial allowances for the purchase of cots/ beds/ bedding/ high chairs/ car seats, although in theory these belong to the county or borough and are reclaimable by them; but in practice I have never once been asked to return anything.

Extras come unasked-for at birthdays and Christmasses. Extras come, if you beat at the door, in regard to sheets for persistent bed-wetters, replacement or repair of worn-out and/or vandalized goods. Currently, for example, I have a 4-year-old who will not leave the car alone – scratches across paintwork, removal of any handy unscrewables, sabotage of child-proof lock mechanism. Very occasionally you can get a sort of educational windfall in the shape of conference/lecture fees such as the annual NFCA weekend, which is worth pushing for because of the stimulating talks, discussions, workshops, and appropriate occupations and pastimes for children.

These payments may look like money for jam to the non-fostering outsider. They complain that rates are scattered like confetti when, of course, everybody knows that it doesn't cost all that much to keep a child. But a fostered child isn't just any child; he is in need of special care, special protection, special understanding and an extra-special ration of parental time. A child living in a Home costs up to eight times the sum of a fostering allowance. Indeed, the child living in a Home for up to one year costs the taxpayer as much as it would to purchase a couple of terrace houses in, say, Lincolnshire . . . or a little island off the west coast of Scotland.

Fostered children are not eligible for the government Child Benefit, though the handicapped person over the age of two years is, after a pretty rigorous medical examination, able to draw Attendance Allowance. This may be followed up, in cases where there is a marked inability to walk, by another critical medical examination at five years. The Mobility Allowance, which is very generous, is then given to those who fail the test. A free pint of milk a day comes to those who apply (DHSS) for a child under sixteen who, for any reason bar truancy, does not attend school for a significant period.

To critics who gasp at these extras, I would point out that foster parents, because of their total commitment to

71

their children, are not able to take up and put down even a part-time or temporary job to tide them over hard times. Fostering is binding – and restricting.

National Insurance contributions are not much of a worry for the married couple as the husband's NI covers his wife and family, including fostered children. Single foster parents would be wise to pay, off their own bat, Class 2 contributions, which in addition to medical safeguards meets their retirement pension. It does not, however, make any allowance for Unemployment or Sickness Benefit.

As far as income tax is concerned, the news on the whole is good. Straight maintenance is disregarded by the tax man and it is not necessary to declare it on your tax return. However, if you receive what is termed a reward element – which means cash left over after paying out for extras for which you have claimed to care for a very difficult or handicapped child – this handful of gold-dust must be declared.

Your agency (county or borough or voluntary society) will, annually, send you a resumé of the payments you receive. It falls into three parts. There is a basic boarding-out allowance, an additional reimbursement of costs, and a reward payment. Where the fosterers are a married couple, it is customary for the reward element to be entered as 'wife's earnings', so it is unlikely that any tax will be taken, unless the wife has a sizable personal income of her own.

Expenses met by foster parents rather than by the basic allowance, and may therefore be claimed against tax, are negotiable with the tax inspector. Here is a sample of the kind of expenses which qualify. Travel expenses in respect of runaway teenagers (and others); costs incurred by increasing size of family vehicle to transport additional children; extra clothing for children who are habitually destructive or pick threads (children, more especially disturbed children, will pick their clothes, nappies, bedding to pieces, thread by thread.) Extra clothing for children who are fast-growing or obese; gifts and 'rewards' for children needing encouragement; club membership/tuition fees for special interests or activities; hospitality for children's own family; additional insurance premium; increased housing costs; telephone costs; fees met by foster parents in relation to conferences, meetings. I could go on.

There is no need to keep a detailed account of all your spending. Nobody expects to see an account book at the end of each financial year, but it is wise to keep receipts of any large sums expended, to make a note of significant mileage, and to be aware of those smaller sums which recur 'unnoticed'.

Fostering, however you look at it and in whatever style you choose to run your domestic affairs, does not come cheap. The heady days when it was thought adequate to do it for love are gone, thank heaven.

The matter of insurance for fosterers also requires comment. Now that a highish percentage of difficult children, defined as those who have been through the courts or have been in trouble as a result of vandalism and so on, are being placed with ordinary families, the risk element has escalated.

Many authorities take care of any eventuality by making arrangements with their own insurers to extend cover to foster families. Some do not, so it is of the utmost importance to find out whether you are protected by your authority for the foster children or whether the onus to insure lies with you. In either case, you have to inform your insurer that you are foster parents, and if any among you have been involved in, say, arson or theft.

Sometimes it is wise to specify certain items of value which you treasure, even if you belong to the optimistic brigade which imagines that nasty things happen only to other people. The 17-year-old who set our house on fire

burned my collection of literary manuscripts from the
1930/1940 period and there was no redress. However,
had those papers been mentioned on the household
insurance policy, things would have been very different.
Remember that an increased premium directly related to
fostering can be claimed from your local authority.

CHAPTER 5

How to set about fostering;
the rules and regulations

So, having taken all this on board and seen some of
the pros and cons, if you still want to join in and
become foster parents, how do you go about it? The first
step, after application, is vetting, which in certain lights
sounds a bit hard. Yet would-be foster parents acquiesce,
usually indeed with alacrity, and submit themselves to
this detailed examination with a willingness few others
would put up with. The physical and the psyche are taken
apart thread by thread, categorized, praised or winced at
and opinions are committed to black and white, to lie
forever on file.

Form F, which will be produced by your social worker,
provides the guidelines and is used for applicants both for
fostering and adoption. It is treated as totally confidential
by everyone involved in its compilation. It constitutes the
groundwork required before any proposal may go forward
to a panel for approval or disapproval. No reasons are
necessarily given should any applicants fail.

Form F is unevenly divided between fact and opinion.
Material assets, interests and skills on the one hand,
a descriptive overview of the home and family on the
other. Today applicants are encouraged to help fill in
this form, so that an element of fairness prevails and
nobody is left wondering what's been put down as gospel.
Information must be supplied to support statements such
as 'house-proud' or 'has a casual attitude towards neatness
and order'.

Ethnic origin, religious adherence, occupation and

income from all sources will do for kick-off: then names, sex, birth date, relationship (birth, adoption, half, step) and type of school attended by existing children. Older children who have flown the nest, dead or alive, also feature. What have they done, are doing, propose to do? How do all these children view any proposed addition to their numbers? Adult members of the family, live-in grannies and so on, are interviewed personally and their opinions sought. Friends, neighbours, godparents, aunts and uncles and so on; if any are hostile to fostering, how are applicants going to cope with that hostility? Unwillingness to accept strange blood does exist. Indeed, on occasion it does amongst my own more distant relatives, who may say, 'we pay our dues in order that folk like that can shirk their responsibilities while people like you look after their offspring. Except, naturally, when it suits them to have those children home for the odd weekend.'

Skeletons long folded away in family cupboards may be exposed and dusted down; grandma's senile dementia, auntie's three grown-up children of limited mental grasp, Dad's brother who's done time for embezzlement. Other family history such as asthma, heart murmurs and emotional aberrations must also come out at the confessional. Anything, in fact, that might conceivably affect the new and as yet unknown child.

A thumbnail sketch of each family member has to be given with details of physical appearance and temperament and natural background. Were you, indeed, fostered or adopted, abandoned in a railway station waiting room or brought up by a single mother on a boot-string? Talents are proudly displayed; arty, computer wizard, Olympic swimmer. Needs are noted: the need for family support; the need to work full-stretch; the need for occasional escapes from domestic turmoil in order to re-charge; the need for the odd tot of whisky. What are the relationships between certain members of the family? Are there favourites like 'Mummy's girl' and 'Daddy's boy'?

Significant relationships have to be laid bare; are they on-going or did they exist before marriage or cohabitation? Why, if they did, did they collapse, what has happened to the children of such unions? Documents concerning separation, divorce, care and control, custody and maintenance must be provided.

Notes are made about the numbers of times applicants are seen, together or separately, by the relevant social worker, as well as on any additional interviews with, say, referees and the comments they offered.

British Agencies for Adoption and Fostering publishes the standard medical form relating to the examination of applicants. It looks very deep and leaves no particle of the body unturned. It also costs. Some boroughs meet the fee; don't forget to nudge the social worker on this point because for the two of you the bill could be heavy. Even if nothing further comes of your application, you at least have the satisfaction of knowing your physical strengths and weaknesses.

Local authority enquiries must now be made to establish if there are any known irregularities. Have you used your house for questionable purposes, been the recipient of repeated bailiff's orders, have the dustbin men refused to collect because you've thrice left out unwrapped and unmentionable matter in large quantities? Checks are made with the police with the dates of any reports received. The social services department is not much concerned over the fact that you've been done for a bald tyre in 1979 or made a request for an extended drinks licence at the village hall on account of your silver wedding party. The ruling powers would, however, draw in a deep breath should you, or your partner, or the live-in granny have been involved in any case of child neglect, prostitution, GBH, indecent exposure or similar happenings. Just occasionally some terrible truths, hidden carefully from a loving and trusting spouse for years, are dug up and hung out to air.

The members of the decision-making panel will want to know whether your house is mortgaged, rented or paid for; they will want to know about your neighbourhood's ethnic mix, its schools, sports facilities and transport. If you have a car who drives it? They do not ask whether the children would have seat belts in the back, or if you carry a first aid kit or if you've ever been in an accident caused by you. They want to know about your work, your spouse's work, and its position in your priorities. Your social life: are you as a family stand-offish; are you joiners of organizations, protesters, the mainstay of under-dogs; do you wear your sense of altruism on your metaphorical cap like a Salvationist's badge; or do you, in the opinion of your inquisitor, go about your ways quietly and without expectation of acknowledgement?

Towards the end of Part One of Form F, as a sort of summing-up, the type of resource you may or may not be able and willing to offer is submitted for consideration. In the event of a long-term placement, for instance, would your family be willing to make the shift from fostering to legal adoption? Would finances permit this, or would you put in for an adoption allowance from your council, or would you be willing to opt for the more recently introduced custodianship (a sort of leasehold adoption)? Would you, whether fostering or taking rights over the child(ren) further, feel happy about parental contact, or contact with the wider natural family, grandparents, aunts, etc.?

If for one of a thousand reasons you feel that your debut into the exacting world of fostering must, at least to start with, be taken in short and probably hectic bursts, there are further sub-divisions to consider. 'Time limited' is the term now applied to what used to be called temporary. Never use one word where two or three will do. In fostering, time limited is generally deemed to apply to any placement of six months or less. It may be as long as 180 days: it may be as short as 24 hours. Time limited includes emergencies such as a parent taken ill or being injured; abandonment; lightning action required as a result of the urgent removal of a child (this papers over the probable name-change of the current place-of-safety. A rose by another name); respite care or a desperately-sought landing-ground for an impossible teenager or an explosive and unappealing younger child.

The prospective fosterers have every right to stipulate age range, gender and the number of children they think they can accommodate; whether or not they feel up to coping with mentally or physically handicapped or emotionally haywire children; whether, indeed, there is any inability to feel wholly at ease on account of racial background, of incest, of the sins of the fathers.

Part Two of Form F deals with further facts of a more personal nature. Be prepared to speak of your infertility without a lump in the throat, tell the interviewer how you've coped with the emotions of being childless, if you are, and what, if any, treatment you've undergone: tubes blown, the tiresome temperature chart, drugs, AIH. Tell them the lot.

If you've consciously decided to limit the size of your family, say how you came to feel that it wasn't necessary for you to have a baby every year like in the pre-Stopes days and whether the decision was unilateral or bilateral. Go back to your own family's background; class, style, circumstance of creation, education and standards. The objective interviewer will want to sound you out on residual bitterness, regrets or remorse and excavate any holes which may point to laxity, transgression or rejection.

Why, you will be obliged to ask yourself, do you want to take on somebody else's child, even if only for a short space of time, in preference to having another of your own? If you insist that you are prepared to study for the privilege, are you really willing to put yourself out to attend tailored courses? And what will happen to the rest of the family while you are out pursuing that knowledge? What, in a nutshell, do you expect to get out of this deal? Love, money, satisfaction, fulfilment or, God forbid, a job? And what will the children make of that?

The Child Care Act, 1980 is our guide book; it is the yardstick by which our children are categorized and channelled; the statutes of law by which we are bound. It is also acknowledged to be one of the most messy, convoluted, incomplete and unintelligible documents ever to have been produced. Professionals and laymen alike are confused by its rhetoric.

The 1980 Act does not purport to be other than, in the main, an amalgam. Parts of 22 previous Acts are incorporated, including pertinent points from as far back as The Children and Young Persons Act of 1933. The most important stems supporting current legislation are represented by the two mammoth Acts of 1948 and 1975. The 1963 and 1975 Acts, though hardly insignificant, have left their marks less obtrusively upon the statutes of which we are gradually becoming more cognizant.

As working foster parents we are not required to digest every last clause of the 1980 or other relevant Acts. However it makes sense to understand opinions and positions which do, or may, concern us, now or in the future, with reference to our children and their status in law. Children themselves, remember, carry no political weight; they have no vote, so we, as their guardians in the broad sense, must endeavour to comprehend what is on offer on their behalf.

We begin with the Boarding-out Regulations of 1955. This covers the duties of what is called the placing authority on the one hand and the undertakings to be agreed by foster parents on the other. So note that the seemingly innocuous form, signed soon after (repeat, after) the acceptance into your home of any given child, constitutes a legal obligation and will be treated as such in certain negative situations. I write of the Foster Parent Agreement document (*see* p. 95) which binds us to promising to care for a child as our own, yet lower down on the page promising with equal vigour to 'allow the child to be removed from the foster home when so requested by a person authorized by the council'.

A nation-wide peace-time social conscience did not really surface in Britain until the late 1940s. With the death of a boy at the hands of his West Country foster parents, public opinion, thanks to pressure from the popular press, demanded better and stricter rules and conditions to safeguard children forced by circumstance to live away from their own homes and families.

Although we are told in general terms why any child we are offered is being taken into care, it does not necessarily follow that we are also told into which specific category of care as outlined in the 1980 Act that child falls. Sometimes, indeed, one type of order is superseded by another, sliding the safety of a child onto a stronger footing.

Most children enter care under Section 2 of the Act. There are three main causes. a) when there is no parent or guardian; b) when the child is either lost or abandoned; c) when the parent or guardian cannot provide for the child's accommodation, maintenance, and upbringing. This last could be because of the illness or handicap of one or both parents or any other wretched reason for which the parents cannot be blamed. Whatever the cause for removing any child into care, the local authority's social service staff must be convinced that it is in the interest and welfare of the child that he should be separated, in material and practical matters, from his past.

Such a situation is known as voluntary care. Indeed it is not at all out of the ordinary for parents themselves to request that a child be placed with foster parents because they cannot cope with him at home. However under Section 2 it remains an obligation, mostly in theory so far as I understand it, to try to return the child to his birth-family if it would be consistent with his well-being. This piece of legislation can be interpreted every-which-way. Under Section 2 a child may, with provisos, be removed from care by his parents should they see fit to insist on doing so; in any event he is discharged from care as soon as he reaches his eighteenth birthday.

Section 3 of the 1980 Act embraces those cases where longer-term care within a foster family or community home is often envisaged to last throughout childhood and is deemed a sensible decision regarding a child already placed with one or the other under Section 2. It is at this point that the local authority may take parental rights and powers over a child, thus removing those prerogatives from the natural progenitors. There are categories under which this legislative power may be implemented.

a) if both parents are dead and there is no appointed guardian.
b) if the parents have abandoned the child or suffer permanent disability so that they are unable to take reasonable care. Likewise if the parents suffer a mental disorder rendering adequate care out of the question. Likewise if the parents practise certain habits resulting in a mode of life which render them unfit for the rearing of a child or if the parents have persistently failed without reasonable cause to discharge their obligations to care for a child.
c) where the child has been in care for a continuous period of at least three years.

Parents in all the above categories have full rights to object to the proposal of withdrawing their right to control their child's life. If they do, the case passes to the juvenile court for a decision. In the main, however, the relevant council has the unilateral right to decide where a child shall be fostered, to deny his natural parents the opportunity to have him at home with them and, though this happens rarely, to block their right to visit.

However, as with most rules, provision is made for them to be cancelled if and when conditions or events change for the better. That is, there is no guarantee that absolute security up to the age of eighteen can ever be watertight. The child you have fostered cannot, even with custodianship, be regarded as immovable. In most Section 3 cases he does turn out to be so, but don't count on it.

An emergency order lies behind precipitate placements, which are often required during a weekend, after office hours or even in the middle of the night. The local authority is responsible for closely examining situations or incidents of abuse where a child is in danger of being hurt. The law provides the authority with powers for the child to be taken forthwith to a place of safety which is often a foster home. There are occasions when mother can come too, as I know well. Father could be the worse for drink, for instance, and having a go at both of them.

Applications for this time-restrictive order can be made to a JP at any time, day or night, or to any sitting court. Investigations which may involve the police, the health and welfare services, even the NSPCC, will lead to a decision about the best action to be taken for the future of the child. Should he, indeed, be returned home, or should an application be made to the juvenile court for a Supervision Order or a full Care Order?

The child coming into your home on such an emergency basis can be jolly hard work. He is hurt within and without, plunged without warning into a strange house with strange people and probably on the wave of an almighty rumpus at home. Above all he is frightened, and neither he, nor you, nor the world at large, knows for sure whither he is going. Be gentle with him, however much he may kick you.

Other children are driven to our door by their social worker in the wake of a Care Order. The magistrate acted because of one or more of six possibilities:

a) that the child's development is being avoidably prevented or neglected; or his health is being avoidably impaired or neglected; or he is being ill-treated.

b) that it is probable that the relevant condition in a) will be satisfied since it has already been satisfied with regard to another child of the same household.

c) that the child is exposed to moral danger.

d) that the child is beyond parental, or other, control.

e) that the child is truanting or being kept from school for other avoidable reasons and is thus not receiving full-time education.

f) that the child is guilty of an offence which would, were he adult, be classed as criminal, while at the same time it would seem unlikely, in the opinion of the court, that suitable supervision and care would be forthcoming at home.

Section 7 of the Act would seem to be pretty closely allied to f) above. Any child aged ten or over may be committed by the court to the care of his local authority if he is found guilty of an offence which would have been punishable by imprisonment had he been of age. A marked lack of parental care would add weight to this decision.

Care Orders may be dropped on application to the court by the council, the child's parents or by the child himself should circumstances improve. In all other cases it is effective until he reaches his majority (eighteen) or until the age of nineteen if the original Care Order had been made after his sixteenth birthday.

In fairness, it must be said that children and young people who are brought into care after really unsociable behaviour has set in are generally placed, if not in a community home specially geared for incomers of their type, then with thoroughly trained and prepared 'professional' foster parents. These diehards are not, like us, coping with a family of mixed ages, mixed levels of intelligence and mixed ranges of development. It is highly unlikely, but not unheard of, that the easily-led and vulnerable will be forced to rub shoulders with those who are sorely in need of reform. It is rare that common-or-garden fosterers are offered the real hard-liners.

The muddled, the emotionally confused, the pickers and fibbers and tell-tales, the molested and abused, the unspeakably dirty, the little wild animals slither in among our darlings, and find their place, or sometimes fight against doing so, with varying degrees of cooperation. But the real bruisers, seldom if ever.

It is useful for foster parents to know how children stand, in the eye of the law, if offences are committed. Any child who has passed his tenth birthday but not yet reached his seventeenth can be charged or reported by the police. Every area force has a Juvenile Liaison Officer who may visit a family in times of crises, collate their findings with those of the relevant social services and, only then, decide on their course of action. The ultimate decision, whether to prosecute or merely to caution, is taken by the Crime Prosecution Service.

If a fostered child is taken to a police station, both foster parent(s) and the social services should be informed and, if the child asks for you to be present when he is questioned or asked to give a statement, you have a right as a 'responsible adult' to be there with him. Cases which cannot be prevented from going to court and which may lead to prosecution are heard by the magistrates in the juvenile courts where special sessions deal with young offenders only.

Though classed as a responsible adult with regard to your foster child, do remember that you are not his next of kin. If he is under a Care Order and parental rights have been taken over by the county or borough council, then it is those authorities who are his legal guardians and next of kin. In all other cases the natural parents retain those rights.

If your child runs away or is in any other way absent without reasonable explanation, the social services, or duty officer if the wanderer scarpers after office hours, must be notified and it is they who are required to contact the police.

Once I lost a child late at night. One dreary November, padding round the bedrooms, checking that they were asleep and covered up, I found Richard's bed cold and empty. He was not in the loo, nor in the kitchen tucking into a midnight snack, nor comfortable in anyone else's bed. In a minor panic I roused the other five children. Had Richard spoken of being unhappy, of going home, of striding out into the world to seek his fortune? No. We searched the house from tiles to foundations: we searched the stable (goat), the hen pen, the dog's house, inside the car and among all the wheelbarrows and bags of peat in the sheds. The 10-year-old had evaporated. Clothing from yesterday was still in its untidy heap on the bedroom floor; his shoes, even his slippers and dressing gown where where he had thrown them. Was he out in the grey sleet in his little cotton pyjamas?

The policemen arrived and repeated the house-search, the garden-search and the buildings-search. Every byway of the village was combed, every hedge poked with a stick and peered behind. Richard's stepfather was knocked up from his bed and urged to help scour the route from our house to his, a distance of some five miles. As desperation heightened, time passed and the night grew more bitter, sniffer dogs were despatched from their resting place many miles away.

Meanwhile one of my grown-up sons arrived to help. He

thrashed through yet another search, heaved out clothes and furniture and the rubbish from the attics.

Then he started on the airing cupboard . . . Richard lay, had lain throughout the shouting and running of feet, fast asleep at the back of that long cupboard, right against the wall and nestled into the untidiness like a bug in a blanket. When my son lifted him out of this camouflaged nest he did not wake; as I tucked him into his bed he opened one eye a mere crack and mumbled 'go away'. The sniffer dogs were bidden to make a U-turn midway: the policemen had tea and two-and-a-half packets of ginger biscuits. The bewildered stepfather returned to his neat maisonette. All the wakened children withdrew to their unfinished dreams. The incongruity of this non-event prompted nervous laughter, but the policemen swept it aside, as just part of the work they expected to get from time to time, with the generosity of thankful relief.

At breakfast time Richard listened, fascinated, to the story of his disappearance. All he remembered was getting up, going to the bathroom and . . . then the morning.

It may be a comfort to those of us who panic easily to know that the great majority of small or smallish children who do the vanishing trick are found to have been at home all the time and, like Richard, to have dropped into a deep sleep in some unsuspected or deeply concealed place.

It is also true that most parents instinctively call on the help of the police rather than remember to conform to the rule of contacting the social services first. It has something to do, I feel, with the concept of wasted time. Certainly, throughout Richard's hibernation in the airing cupboard, I never once gave a thought to the duty officer.

A child may, while staying with you, be made a Ward of Court. This means that he, being under the guardianship of the court, is required to remain where he is until a further directive is received. In all likelihood he has come from a hazardous background and his future is uncertain. You, his proxy parents, represent his only hope of security, but only for the time being. As the people closely involved with a confused and possibly rebellious child, you will understand that he has to stay with you because the magistrate has ordered this for the child's safety. The local authority has dealt with all the initial work, has weighed up the desirability of wardship, has coped with the paperwork, the interviews and the court but it is the foster parents who pick up the broken pieces and attempt the patching job. Where there is a possibility of the natural parent, or anyone else, removing the child, a sense of super-precaution must take over. You must make the old adage, 'he's never out of my sight for a moment', be as true as ever it will be. This is an anxious and stressful burden to carry, because you are at one remove from the events which led to the child being made a ward. You are more involved than anyone else in the everyday practicalities of the protection and in the ongoing loving and caring necessary to keep the child unruffled though informed of what is happening.

It is awesome to know that it is the court, and the court alone, which has the power to decide in which direction the child's destiny lies. The local authority, or whoever else has taken the wardship step, has surrendered the ultimate responsibility. You, the foster parent, are merely a caretaker. If it is considered right for the child to go to the other end of the world, then you are obliged to acquiesce. Saying goodbye to a wardship child can be quite a wrench for both of you.

You must also file away into the bottom drawer of your mind the possibility of a situation known popularly as the 'tug of love'. In fostering, this emotional phenomenon doesn't come about as often as you might be led to believe but there are circumstances where a child might be required to move on against your wishes. Such was Kenneth, a boy of five who, for two years, had been loved, cared for, nursed and allowed to capture the hearts of a young couple prepared to give over whole sections of their life to him. The local authority was concerned that the foster parents had become too wrapped up in the boy, too protective, too much inclined to give in to be good for his potential; they removed him and gave him to us.

What, I wonder now, became of you, Kenneth? Within our supposedly normal family we taught you to be clean and to feed yourself, to totter a few blind steps and, just once, to say 'goat'. But we could not spare you all the time you wanted, could not manage the lifting and physical control you needed as the years went by.

Whether, throughout that time, you bonded with us I don't know; the concentration of your being was directed inwards and distracted us from our other, less burdened, children. So we let you go back to the sorting house at the age of eight because we could not do well enough by you. I have wondered since how the original too protective, too doting pair who suffered the tug of love on your account would have viewed our failure?

Then there are the tugs set in motion when a natural parent reclaims a child after a change of heart or mind or circumstance. Under present legislation a so-called 'snatch-back' must, in the case of a child fostered under Section 2, be preceded by a period of 28 days' notice. Release from care is then allowed so long as the authorities are satisfied with events.

In the old days a child considered to be in voluntary care could be collected by a parent almost at whim. An impulsive act instigated perhaps by the break-up of a love affair or a little well of self-pity was, frequently, merely a forerunner to *Angst* and bitterness and fight. Foster parents would cry out in genuine anguish blaming the law for its lack of feeling when children they had come to love were summarily removed.

I write, of course, of the extremes, of the emotional maelstroms which hit the headlines and sometimes even the TV news with heart-wrenching quotes and pictures geared to affect even the sturdiest hearts. But that type of instant snatch-back lies, except in cases of private fostering, well in the past.

Today, any child whom you have fostered for six months or longer is, even under a voluntary agreement where the actual rights are still vested in the natural parents, protected in law. Any natural parent wishing to restore a child to his first home must inform the local authority in writing of his or her wish to do so. All parties benefit from this sensible bit of legislation. The relevant social worker is given time to unravel/ placate/ pour oil/ instil a modicum of common sense/ counsel/ defend (or oppose)/ befriend/ badger/ or suggest a resort to law. The parent has time to think deep and hard, to consider next month and next year as well as the immediate urge for family reunion. An impulsive demand for the return of a child (sometimes a child who was found difficult to manage when at home before) can be seen more realistically in the period this safety-gap gives. A heart-to-heart talk with the social worker sometimes results in more frequent and/or flexible visiting arrangements which, to a muddled or so-called inadequate parent, can lessen the ache of loss while ensuring that the child himself remains settled.

The foster parent must find time, at this threatened disruption of the *status quo*, both to see the predicament of the natural mother, or father, or both, and genuinely to look at the child's situation, practical, emotional, developmental, from an objective point of view. What is best for the child must be recognized. To stay or to go? Honesty is sometimes clouded in the face of anger or anxiety or sheer fear of loss. There are times when a foster mother has to ask herself whether she is really the only person who could satisfactorily bring up this child or that. There are children who, however neglected or confused or messed about by a natural parent, remain bonded to her as though drawn by a magnet. Sometimes we have to let go.

Of course the 28 days' notice can be used as a period of fierce legal activity. There are, for example, many cases where a child has been left in care under Section 2 for years. All has seemed safe; the parents have visited and continued to take a fairly healthy interest; the early years of tantrums, school phobia and a reluctance to take to clean habits are over; the firm but sensible handling of a foster parent has at last resulted in a thoroughly passable 10-year-old. Yet his consuming nervousness is only buried skin-deep. He will need years more of the same consistent care if he is to hold his own in the world as a young man. To return home to a harsher lifestyle, one where it may be necessary for survival to fight for certain privileges, could plunge a tender child into a terrible regression.

He himself, dizzy with hints and innuendoes, anxious for the pot of gold at the end of the rainbow, can't wait. Yet at the same time he is aware that there may be a darker side. Could he not be supplied with 10p pieces so that he could ring up if he needs to be fetched home? Home? And what if the boy in the top flat bullies him again? And do I know the best way of not looking at something you don't like, something frightening, without actually appearing to have the eyes shut?

The right place for such a child must be protected throughout his period of growth. The hard work of years can be smashed within a matter of weeks by too precipitous a return home. Parents, however ready they may feel about taking on their little problem again, are generally malleable in the face of compassionately presented reason. Every point of the child's potential, his future, his weaknesses and his reliance on the familiar must be rationalized and sifted and viewed from every angle before an unplanned change is agreed. His needs and the growth of his personal independence are more important, at least for the time being, than any ideal reunification within a family group.

Foster parents, who know the child better than anyone else, have every opportunity to make their feelings known to anybody in a position to influence the final decision. Wardship, in a difficult case, could well be the answer, followed by the court's recommendation of a long overdue Care Order which would remove the parental rights. This in no way affects their right to visit as formerly or indeed more frequently, nor their right to have the child home with them when he leaves care.

Foster parents have other rights in law. After three years' continuous care of a child the foster family is entitled without hindrance to apply to the court for custody. If a Custodianship Order goes through, then nobody may remove that child from the foster home without further resort to the court.

This situation remains permanent as long as your good standards of care continue and the natural parents are satisfied with the *status quo*. The child, although not legally yours as is one born of your body, now has the right to a secure childhood which can only be reversed through the courts.

After a period of five years or more in the continuous care of one foster family those who have, in all practical ways, acted as parents may simply apply to the courts to adopt the child. Between the time of your application and the magistrate's decision the child may not be removed from your home. Everyone concerned will get the opportunity to put their opinions for and against and to make decisions about the continuance or otherwise of natural parents' visits, and the question of finance. If the judgement is in your favour, then the child becomes, in every particular save that of physical birth and the right to inherit a title, your own. Out of care for good, and into yours.

On the other side of the adoption question we have a situation which is often left to the fosterers as far as explaining the moves to the children is concerned. Suppose, for example, you have a couple of little girls who have been abandoned by their single mother. She has made it plain to the authority that, for many reasons, she cannot take care of her daughters nor does she see herself ever reaching a stage when a stable, affectionate home would be available to them. She is not 'given to motherhood' and knows they would be better off with people who could really be parents to them. She volunteers to make the break easier by not visiting them while the fostering placement fills the gap between being received into care and an adoptive family materializing.

Who is going to tell the girls? At four and six they are too old for adoption to be arranged without their knowledge, too young to take on board the emotional implications of their mother's decision. While she has told them in her own manner that she is going away their comprehension of time-scale precludes any conception of forever. An official 'sit down, I have something to tell you' approach does not work with such young children. Often they do not or cannot pay attention; they do not recall accurately or even in the correct context as shattering a revelation as 'Mummy won't be able to have you home with her any more'. They cannot accept the truth, for with all her failing and vacillations they love her.

They talk about her.

'Mummy didn't do it this way. She put the cheese in first, then cooked it.'

'When we were at home we stayed up late with Mummy when she wasn't feeling very well. We made her a drink and gave her some medicine and a cigarette.'

'We weren't allowed marmalade at Mummy's house. She said it was only for grown-ups. Is it really all right for us to have some?'

They express anxiety about the length of time since they saw their mother; ask when she is going to visit. They see the other fostered children in the family visited by their parents, so this is natural. 'Why doesn't she write?' The other children receive post-cards or are telephoned.

One fudges for a little while. 'Mummy is feeling a bit muddled; she's sorting herself out.' 'Mummy's not on the 'phone any more, not since she's moved house.' 'Mummy's got a new job and probably feels awfully weary in the evenings so has put off writing letters.'

We know, the social worker knows, the mother and her boy-friend and her family know; yet those on centre stage live in hope in a misty fairyland, unable to understand that their mother will never return. We must wait for the opportune moment; for a likely opening when their small minds would seem receptive.

This moment occurred in our local supermarket recently. The smaller child, deliberating upon the choice of cereals, wistfully wondered if her mother ever would come to see them; not, please note, whether her mother would ever come to take them home. Both girls were with me and I felt instinctively that the time was right. So there, adjacent to the Shredded Wheats, they learned of mother's withdrawal and their own prospect of adoption.

The rules in such predicaments are these. Never, however you may feel about the matter, paint a natural parent in a bad light; select your words carefully and use language the children can understand; finish your story optimistically so that the child may build on it towards the new life ahead.

My little girls could understand that their mother was all mixed up because they had seen her so. The fact that she had decided it was too much for her to look after them any more was put into context by the good news that they would soon be getting a new Mummy and Daddy. This couple would be chosen specially for them, would love them more than anything in the world and would keep them as their own daughters for always and always.

In our case I spoke of my own older children, adopted by me years ago; about how they were before they became 'mine', living in a children's home and waiting for their 'new Mummy'. I took care to stress that the girls would stay with me and the family until their special parents were found. Later, my grown-up children were able to tell the little girls about what being adopted was like so that they understood the meaning of the word and its broader implications.

Excitement and looking forward thenceforth took precedence over yearning for the past and speculating upon the absence of their first mother. Such children, waiting in the limbo between their original family and their projected new family, need a tremendous amount of tender loving care. As temporary fosterers we are tiding these children over. Adoptions, even in the climate of few available infants, often takes many months to arrange.

We ought to end this chapter with a few paragraphs about the Foster Care Charter and its propagator, the National Foster Care Association (NFCA).

Founded in 1974, the Association was set up specifically to help and inform parents with extended families of this kind. It has over the years grown from a small voice crying in the social wilderness about lack of knowledge, lack of justice, lack of liaison between the authorities and fosterers, lack of any sort of respect for the job, to a thousands-strong membership drawn from child care professionals and foster parents alike. Nowadays the NFCA has clout, sways establishment opinion, opens dark cupboards. It recognizes the paramount importance of all involved in this deviant family structure of making their views known, their grievances aired, their praises audible to the man in the street.

The Association has adopted a ten-point Charter which, in terms of child care thinking, is right up-to-date. Substitute parenting in relation to the giver, the receiver, the adult, the child, is defined in these rights which run as follows:

1) Foster care is a partnership. Participators are carers, social workers, the placing agency and, if possible and desirable, the child and his natural parents.
2) Respect must be afforded to cultural, racial and religious identities of both cared-for and carers in choice of placement and subsequent support.
3) Effort must be made to establish continuity in a child's life so that his identity may be maintained, his well-being promoted and potential realized.
4) The real cost of supporting a foster child must be met and, in addition, carers should be able to receive a fee for specialized skills.
5) Opportunities for initial and on-going training must be made available, and where necessary funded by the relevant authority, in respect of foster parents, social workers and other professionals involved in this branch of child-care.
6) All who are working within the fostering situation must be able to feel that support from the authority may be begged as needed.
7) The responsibilities shouldered by the authority in direct respect of the foster parents (purposes and goals of each placement) must be stated in writing. Likewise the responsibilities of foster parents in respect of the authority.
8) Important decisions relating to a child in care should, where truly practicable/possible, be made after consultation with the child himself, the natural parents, the foster parents and the social workers.
9) Foster parents, children and their natural parents should have the opportunity to challenge decisions made independently by the fostering authority and be made aware of procedures open to them.
10) It shall be recognized that young people leaving care at eighteen or nineteen have a right to expect further support into adulthood.

At first reading it would seem that all these ten points could, in practice, be adopted without difficulty or hardship. Most, nowadays, are. However, we have a long way to go before being allowed any serious involvement in decisions which affect the natural parents. Appointments with specialists, relief care, police matters, and so on have, in my experience anyway, been taken care of well before the natural parents are informed, if, indeed, they are at all. Perhaps we are afraid of argument, of their not seeing the point or not being able to take on board the real difficulties under which their children labour. But mostly, I think, we are afraid of hurting them. Are we embarrassed because, as ordinary mortals and lucky enough to have grown up without scars, we are able to bring up their children as our own while they have, or have been deemed by other people's standards to have, failed? But when we are all brave enough to put the new code into effect those first parents should (must) be made party to all important decisions, must be told what choices they have and must be given the credit for being able to give a considered answer.

Clause no. 6, again from my experience over the years, is far from being met in reality. Lack of manpower and finance, indeed, preclude any appreciable reduction of pressure. Support in our difficulties with certain children, even when breaking-point is round the corner or the famous 'burn-out' down to the last cold ashes, is seldom available. My family has recently been relieved, on alternate weekends, of a child whose influence on the smaller ones can be pretty awful, but it has taken me two years of consistent whining to bring this about.

Another boy, angry with us and the world and himself and anti-social to the last thread of patience was, apart from brief formalities, left to topple his own world and ours in spite of his two social workers being well aware of the strain under which we were all living. Support, even an understanding glance, an outstretched hand or a sympathetic word, might just have changed my decisions which led me to take the boy to school one day yet request that the social services pick him up and harbour him somehow, almost anyhow, forever after. It was the child-on-the-doorstep routine in reverse; I shifted him from mine.

I certainly can't claim I've never received support from the authorities. There was splendid young Danny, gentleman help and children's friend, who worked for us all through one summer's school holiday and was paid for by the social services. There have been super social workers who have tried their damnedest to help, but of no avail. There have been others who, unable to offer immediate practical help have borne in a punnet of strawberries, a tin of extraordinarily sticky home-made toffee, a couple of fertile goose eggs (for broody Greyback) and other sundry gifts of a placatory nature. But, on the whole, much more back-up is needed if tragic breakdowns, which are mostly avoidable, are to be averted.

Clause no. 9: the right of fosterers, natural parents and/or children themselves to have recourse to challenge decisions made by the authority. Has, to date, any foster parent actually been made aware of 'the procedures whereby they can exercise their right of challenge'? Not I for certain.

Currently, for instance, I am fighting like a tiger against a decision for a parent to say goodbye to a child of four who is destined for adoption. That little boy was thrown off by his first mother over six months ago. He grieved for her long and hard and has been loved and cuddled and talked through his bad times until, now, he is able to trust the world and find enjoyment in play and friendship. What havoc would saying goodbye leave in its wake so far as the child is concerned? In whose interest, I mean, would the parting be held? And who would sweep up the broken pieces?

CHAPTER 6

Damaged children

Damaged is an adjective readily applied to children of all ages coming into or going through care. They are, without exception, casualties of circumstance. Luckily for the human race most of these children's bruises heal: the majority of young animals are as resilient as rubber and have a life force which satisfactorily pushes the past either into oblivion or an acceptable mental pigeon-hole. The few mend quickly, almost before our eyes, as we go about our business around them and with them. Others need almost unlimited time, or therapy, before they can see their world in the right perspective. Some, in one way or another, are destined to remain casualties for life: physical, mental, emotional or, it must be said, behavioural. In almost no circumstance is this damage asked for or self-generated; the fault could be genetic or yesterday's parental rage. However acquired, such damage can render a child's life unalterably different and very often it is the long-term foster parent who, in all practical particulars, patches up the wounds.

Genetic or congenital abnormalities can sometimes be put right, kept in abeyance, masked by drugs, manipulative treatment or stringent supervision. When you accept an infant or young child with a built-in and predictable future you and your partner must go in for some deep mind-searching. This child, now helpless, cuddly, responsive (perhaps) and passively grateful (ditto), will, with a few generally foreseen exceptions, grow up. He will become heavy, maybe physically unattractive, almost certainly frustrated, possibly uncertain in his temperament and could be lacking in socially acceptable graces.

Would you, as a family – your other children will be in on this too, remember – be able to balance the undoubted stress and occasional embarrassment likely to happen against the love you will either receive like a thunderbolt the minute he becomes yours or which will grow imperceptibly with caring? He may shriek out a personal remark such as should only be whispered in the privacy of one's own home; he may exhibit a surplus of saliva when taking tea with acquaintances; there may be an accidental puddle in Sainsbury's.

The child could be with you into adulthood even though fostering officially finishes at eighteen; and the pressure will not lessen. And if your own best interests, because of ageing or a greater independence of the young person involved, make change imperative, could you let go with magnanimity?

Damaged children in this category include a fair percentage of those with Down's Syndrome and other such handicaps. Children so affected can, as we all understand, vary one from the other very widely in educational and social goals. All give love unrestrainedly; all are given to moodiness at best, to outbursts more likely. They will participate in family activities and day-to-day chores; will enjoy being helpful and be pleased with little things.

A typical notice in newspaper or magazine, searching with quiet desperation for a suitable family, could read 'X is a lively and boisterous girl who enjoys playing and dancing. Her strong and determined personality makes her very difficult to manage so she needs a firm hand and constant supervision. She responds best to a disciplined and structured routine, administered by adults as she doesn't get on well with other children. X is partially deaf, with only a limited grasp of sign language. We are looking for a couple with the right degree of firmness and tolerance, living in an area with good special schools and support services for the handicapped. X was rejected by her natural parents as a baby and there will be no contact with relatives.'

Another reads: 'Y was born with spina bifida which was corrected at the age of 18 months. She is enuretic. She is young for her age, attends a special school which she enjoys, but can be very dramatic on occasions. She has tantrums and needs consistent, confident parents who can help her feel good about herself. Although sad and difficult things have happened to Y, she has great affection for her family and wants to stay in touch with them. A tremendous challenge for the right couple.'

Or, almost certainly a rubella child: 'Z is profoundly deaf, partially sighted and developmentally delayed. No contact with natural parents since birth. Generally contented and easy-going; likes to be outdoors and swims well. Walks well, is able to dress himself apart from buttons. Manages unattended at mealtimes and for toilet. Needs a family, couple or single person who would have an overall commitment to him. As he is unable either to speak or hear, it is important that people who consider this 5-year-old are able to offer real security.'

The above samples did not need to be searched for. They represent a mere thread from a huge tangle of family-less children. Children who, failing miracles, look into a future where supervision, assistance and close human ties are part and parcel of existence. Their very condition demands much, much more than most humdrum foster parents can give without foreshortening their own claims of conscience. Requests as set out here are typical of those which elicit no replies at all. This is not because those registered to foster fall short of saintliness, but because heart-searching and common sense reach realistic conclusions about the amount of time, energy, commitment and support required. To be honest, any child beyond babyhood, burdened with major handicaps which necessitate constant and continued assistance, may be considered lucky if a loving family is found where warm integration may still be a possibility.

On the other hand, with an infant of three years or less with similar problems, the response will improve to the point of near certainty. The tiny child presents its handicaps less directly. Lack of speech, sight, hearing; feeble muscle tone, double incontinence, wobbly legs; these imperfections, as with (in some conditions) looks, become more marked with age and growth and progress.

Foster parents, knowing that time and that magical bonding which grows between family and acquired child favour the baby or young toddler, are far more eager to respond to the idea of such a son or daughter. My own youngest, Ben, who suffers from the rare Prader Willi Syndrome, came to us as a very backward 18-month-old and with a prognosis dire enough to make one gasp. He will never sprint for the county, never, indeed, 'walk tall'; his comprehension and concentration may not come up to scratch; his constant, insatiable and uncontrollable quest for food threatens his lease of life; his incomplete nether regions render sexual development, and almost certainly any chance of physical love, beyond even the longest odds. He is ours; he is doted upon for his own sweet self, warts and all. Yet, had this little fellow, with his complex of mental and physical aberrations, been left too long on the home-search file, would we have so readily taken an already obese lad clad in supportive waistcoat and struggling to walk in stout boots with calipers? To my shame I do not care to answer my own question.

Into this same category fall those children whose handicaps, acquired through illness (meningitis, encephalitis, tumours), accident (brain and spinal damage in particular) or gross physical abuse, disrupt own-family caring to such an extent that substitute parenting becomes a desirable alternative.

Child abuse has a sensational connotation. Abuse equals violation and makes good newspaper copy, especially when translated as sexual tyranny. Abuse, which can damage a child *for life*, follows three distinct patterns, all crushingly hurtful in their different ways. There is sadistic hurting for hurting's sake; there is insidious bullying, nagging, criticism, which erodes the child both mentally and emotionally, ruining his self-image and joy; there is sexual interference in all forms from touching up to full rape or buggery. All these abuses are much more likely to be perpetrated by members or close friends of the child's family than by strangers or remoter acquaintances. Lodgers and ill-chosen baby-sitters are not blameless.

Sheer, awful physical brutality, inflicted on a child in temper or frustration, though more understandable than slow and oft-repeated maltreatment, leaves the greater and more lasting mark. A searing rage is dramatic and violent and as a result children on the receiving end can, and do, sustain ruptured organs, internal bleeding, head injuries severe enough to cause mental impairment, even blindness. Broken bones, which are reparable, are almost unimportant by comparison with the long-term devastation caused by inner hurts.

Fathers and stepfathers, mother's boy-friends or live-in lovers are more likely to flail and roar than are the females of the family. The females, usually those who have conceived and delivered the object of their mates' fury, more often than not fail to interfere, fail to join the cry for help, fail to comfort the broken child. In cases of extreme violence male domination is alive and well and would seem to reduce the female partner to the role of mere camp-follower. Even to the point of masking the normally inextinguishable instinct of a mother to protect her young.

These gross outbursts, remember, can be triggered by as little as a wet bed, the failure to eat brussels sprouts, a lost pair of plimsolls or merely being there at all. All some infants need to do is cry because of hunger, discomfort or wind. Sometimes the victim is one of a number of brothers and sisters who is picked on to the exclusion of the others. He may be slower or less attractive or even the sharp one of the brood. Often the cause is not apparent.

Vindictive cruelty, quietly repeated day by day, gradually sucks away the child's personality, identity, will to survive. Again, this subtle cause of unhappiness usually comes from the father-figure, though with the mother's collusion. Withdrawal of treats, extras, of food even, makes a start. The child may find herself in a Cinderella situation if she is deemed lazy, while one who, probably through fear, reverts to dirty habits can be made to live in his own filth. It may be months before a schoolteacher, neighbour or relative notices any tell-tale signs.

Mental or emotional flattening can be achieved on a parallel with the above. A baby who is never played with, spoken to, tickled on the toes or chucked under the chin will, regardless of potential, acquire a non-reactive attitude towards things animate and inanimate. His milestones will fall behind in exact relation to the length of time his sensory perceptions are ignored. Given that the earliest months are of vital learning importance, a lame start, and some lame starts can go on for years, will as easily damage a child as actual physical cruelty.

A child who is always put down or whose lack of achievement elicits adverse comment while hard-come-by achievements are ignored, will cease to make an effort. One who is nagged and picked upon for the most minor imperfection will go one of two ways; he will wait for the next time living on his nerves or he will block off and cease to hear. Being found unacceptable will, with time, erode his own last filament of self-esteem, perhaps for life.

Today there is a new bogey leading to mental disruption. Insulated as we perhaps are, we might be unaware of the uncountable numbers of young children whose minds are regularly bombarded by scenes of most violent and terrifying human behaviour. As a foster mother who, in addition to a permanent family, brought up others' children for the most part to take their pleasures simply and to view horror with horror, I am increasingly made aware of the power of the X video through my contact with incoming temporary children.

To hire a horror movie a person must have reached the age of sixteen, but who exercises any control over who watches the thing at home? Suppose there is no reasonable parent in the home; or one who is of the opinion that nothing ought to be hidden from the modern child?

I have myself seen a 13-year-old boy, formerly of a gentle and polite disposition, changed, in the six months since the family have hired a video machine, into a sadistic bully. The older brothers are out at work and, correctly, maintain that they have the right to spend their own money as they wish. They hire the video, they take out the films and mother has no objection to this material being used for viewing by the rest of the family.

On hearing of a real-life massacre, in which young children were butchered by a madman, this erstwhile tender boy remarked, with some relish, 'Good for him! Great! Just like on the video!' Fed, evening after evening, on scenes of underwater beheadings, squashing of guts, worms in their thousands exuding from every orifice of otherwise everyday human beings, he has, if you like, acquired a taste for the cruelly macabre. His language is foul, his behaviour at school rude and uncaring; 'They can't do anything to me. They can't do a thing. They're not allowed to.' On an access visit he savagely attacked his own father, kicking him to the carpet and booting him in the tenderest parts.

Whether this tendency towards violence and violent thinking is a phase, and as such will pass, remains to be seen. The point is that this boy – and how many others like him? – is beyond control now and is his own man. He is not only damaged by the barbarity but concurrently, and from the same source, has been propelled in the direction of overt and on-going sexual voyeurism. He has seen it all, in full colour and many times. The deprived environment in which he lives encourages this titillation and gratification is not hard to find.

A representative of social services, made privy to the situation, considers the boy's case to be an awkward one. 'Now, if it had been a girl having under-age sex we could be of more help. With this one we'd have to see proof and also see that the child was being harmed by it. Such a lot of these complaints, you see, are made vindictively.'

There is a little brother in this particular family which consists of children all of whom have in the past featured on the at-risk register. There is undoubtedly maternal neglect, physical and emotional, with the older boys shouldering much ostensible responsibility in respect of the youngsters.

Do we, Joe Public, sit back and wait until the balloon goes up? Watch the younger boy, in time, tip over into the same old mess? Or do we attempt to raise our voices, dare I say against the free-for-all of the permissive lobby, on behalf of video sanity? Or do we wait until such as these become our foster children?

Sexual abuse of one kind or another is estimated (MORI poll) to be meted out to 10% of both yesterday's and today's children. For every child who is molested there is also a molester, and that is a tough fact to take on board. Are two out of every ten of us perpetrators or recipients, involved in secret sex? In some cases the root cause is obvious, where sexuality is worn, if I may mix my metaphors, on the sleeve. Children ape what they observe going on around them, and there are families, perhaps only a small minority, where knowledge of sexual intercourse is not considered the prerogative of grown-ups.

More usually (if usually is a decent term to employ) advantage is taken of a child, or children, by one specific member of the family. This advance, if adhering to pattern, makes small beginnings: stroking, tickling, joking playfully with suggestive phrases. Nothing really to shout about except that these games, even so early on, are special between the two participants: a secret. By the time grosser acts are perpetrated the play-acting has been going on too long under hush-hush rules. The child feels guilty, bound by promises, and can often be further shut into silence through fear of reprisals against the abuser – police, prison, break-up of family.

People often don't realize that sexual molestation can begin when the victim is still a baby. Attempts to excite and stretch the tiny genitals can lead to lacerations which, even if the psychological trauma be dispelled, could leave physical scars for life. A small child who has been handled intimately with force will, in reaction, begin to feel safe only when its nappy is snugly fixed. Such a baby will often tense up and scream when the nappy is changed, afraid of its vulnerability.

In-family abuse is not restricted to a liaison between adult male and immature (under sixteen) female. Nor is it the prerogative of one social class or another. B was still at prep. school when his army officer father, a stern disciplinarian much given to administering a whacking and sending miscreants to bed, began to follow up his son's punishment with a visit. B, the not-so-bright child set amid sharp-witted siblings, and an angry child to boot, accepted father's fondlings with a surprise commensurate with the discovery of a soft centre in an otherwise tough world. Repeated visits to the boy's bedroom, with intensified sexual attentions, progressed to full sodomy and variations. Father explained that this was loving and special, but that it must never be talked about.

Because of anal dilation the boy lost partial control of the bowels (a problem which dogged him for life) and, because of his academic backwardness and this loss of control, was sent to a boarding school for children with various handicaps. Neither medical nor psychiatric treatment was of any avail. The boy never had any physical examination of the pertinent part of his anatomy. The truth never came out. Lucky father.

This boy presents a classic example of the damage we must learn to recognize as imposed, not innate. B was obliged to suffer to satisfy his father's pederastic predilections until his late teens, and subsequently made a disastrous homosexual liaison, fell like a stone down the social scale by excessive drinking, gross over-eating and losing all sense of self-preservation. His anti-social behaviour was directed, and he emphasizes that there was nothing subconscious about it, against his father. He'd show him, he'd shame the family name, disgrace the lot; and, by heaven, he did. Yet he never, while his father was alive, told a soul.

This secrecy, partly because the child feels guilty, partly because some things sexual are regarded as rude and thus unmentionable, is very hard to crack. Fear of reprisal has much to do with it; these children have, after all, been made to promise pretty well under oath, and a man, or more rarely a woman, who has been harsh in one area could also prove harsh in another. There is, too, a genuine and deep-seated desperation , belied by a superficial calm, to keep the abuser out of trouble and to keep the family together. This layered thinking is strangely mature and objectively caring far beyond the magpie thought-patterns of childish years; putting the fear and guilt a poor second and third to that of being the manipulator of disintegration.

C, at sixteen an unkempt and painfully shy girl, elected of her own accord to be taken into care because she was unable to get on with mother's boy-friend. For the first eleven years of her life she had been brought up exclusively by mother, together with a younger half-brother. 'I 'ates 'im', constituted her main cry against the man, substantiated by stories of a kitten being burned in the grate, a dog beaten to death, a great clout on the head with a broom and the rule he imposed that reading was forbidden as he was the only one in the house allowed to be literate. Yet her fear and hatred of the man rested, in the main, with the dark secret. He had at first molested her, then, since her maturity, had repeatedly penetrated her. Mother, she was never allowed to forget, had found a good man to take care of her after a long struggle as a single parent. There were by now a further two baby sisters, so in no way was she, C, going to make trouble within that otherwise happy home.

We, removed by many miles from childhood, unscarred by abuse, relatively bold and upstanding on matters which need an airing and, given that we are foster parents, may find it difficult to comprehend this consuming drive on the child's side, to remain silent. Children, on the whole, are such beastly tell-tales; the entire conspiracy to shield their own violator puzzles us.

To some extent all children who come into the arms of a foster family are victims; they are away from their own, making adjustments, removed from the familiar past, however bizarre that past may be. Foster parents grow, with experience, expert at recognizing the types of behaviour which point to repression, bullying, neglect, outright cruelty, though the records do not necessarily specify the background of the child. One child will flinch and even shield his face if so much as approached; another will retract into his world of self-imposed deafness, dumbness, numbness. Overt aggression, with fisticuffs and boots and a wicked tongue; or conversely a servile determination to please. Every child has his own way of mirroring early experiences. So be ready. Much that manifests itself after any child establishes himself in your home may come as a surprise.

The sexually abused child who, far from finding the experience abhorrent, enjoyed it, is more capable than any of administering a metaphorical blow to the solar plexus.

Deprived of it, in all likelihood he misses it. Such a child is invariably superior; he keeps his wicked secret all right, yet he displays in his behaviour that he is not going to give you, or anyone else, the satisfaction of knowing outright.

P, a dapper child of nine, very into stylish dress and hair-do, attentive to his figure ('I wonder if I am the correct weight for my height'), fussing over imagined imperfections of looks or complexion, presented a frankly intimidating picture of an extremely fey young man pint-potted into a little boy's frame. His domination over the younger fostered children in the family soon became evident and supervision was sharpened. Even so, life being what it is, it was a neighbouring parent who gave the red alert concerning his sex games. Her child had been given instruction and had been introduced to the delights of masturbation by P who, she'd been told by her newly-enlightened 8-year-old, 'knew everything'. She had found graphically explicit drawings of both human beings and animals having a whale of a time. She had not liked the tone of the giggling, which was switched off the minute she came upon the scene. She did not, she stated emphatically, wish P to visit her house again.

I have seen a boy of the same age mock up sexual intercourse between a couple of toddlers, urging them on with it, 'That's it – hug her a bit tighter.' That same boy has approached acquaintances and even strangers with almost blatant invitations, needling on till some reaction is elicited. On occasion he still does it.

'Do you think I'm attractive?'

'Why?'

'If I was older would you fancy me?'

Or, on a different tack, aimed perhaps more at embarrassing.

'Are those cows or bullocks?'

'Cows.'

'How do you know?'

'Well, the obvious.'

'I don't know the difference. Tell me how I can see the difference.'

These provocations would seem to be made of gum, stretching on until choked off by either the victim or some outside rescuer.

Even quite little girls will often carry their pattern of formerly expected behaviour into the foster family. Flirting, touching in what the general welfare services like to call 'an inappropriate manner', pulling down their little knicks.

Older girls, those who are not shrinking and hurt, may blatantly make passes, use risky words at which more genteelly-bred mortals blush, roar with suggestive laughter at cucumbers and other such innocent articles, sometimes even make a beeline for the foster father simply for the joy of seeing foster mother jealous.

The abused child may make a point of trying to get into the bathroom when others are having a bath or going to the lavatory. In countless homes all over the world it is all right to swan in and out of the bathroom regardless but with the experienced child there is an excessive urgency to get a good view. He/she will be tapping at the door the minute the hot tap's turned on, the minute you settle on the seat. And that tapping will be of the can't-wait-a-second variety, punctuated with threats of bursting and beggings to open up for mercy's sake.

This trail to the bathroom door is altogether different from that other watchful compulsion exhibited by the nervous child who cannot bear the uncertainty of having you out of his sight. This shadow will wait like an anxious little hound, lonely for your reassuring presence, half-afraid you might never emerge again, living only for the sound of the flush or the gurgle of the waste plug. The joy of returning security. This child, unlike the first, with no interest in catching anyone with his pants down, is a casualty of a quite different mismanagement.

So, in a complex nutshell, we who foster must be ready a) to take on board aberrations other than and in addition to those known about before the child's placement; b) be on the look-out for emotional and behavioural clues which either confirm already-recognized damage or substantiate suspicions; and c) know how best to deal with them from our own, our existing family's and the new child's point of view.

Remember that it is highly unlikely that any social worker involved in the decisions concerning care and placement has had a chance to examine the child thoroughly. It is essential that as early on as possible and certainly before day two has dawned, we take the opportunity to look over the new arrival for signs of physical damage such as bruises, swellings, sores, rashes and minor wounds. A child whose reason for being received into care lies with parental neglect has a high-risk chance of surface hurts. A young child of primary school age or below will almost always agree to have an evening bath, and will thus be open to innocent scrutiny. With an older child, who might be frightened or offended by a gentle inspection, one plays it by ear, never adding insult to possible injury.

However, for the child's good and for your own protection you must report, in writing, any outward and visible marks which could have been made intentionally or which might reasonably be attributable to such severe neglect as, for example, a nappy rash which has caused subcutaneous erosion. The date and time when you first noticed these scars or contusions should be jotted down, for it is not unknown for foster parents themselves to be accused of injuring a child; so take this precaution as a measure of self-protection. Any human being, when up against the wall, may be tempted to throw the blame at any handy recipient and a parent suspected of harsh treatment will take any opportunity of redirecting accountability away from himself.

As a fostering family we must also from time to time watch our own language. I don't mean cursing and swearing but using everyday words and phrases (even the tone of voice) which might have had quite different meanings and innuendoes in the child's natural family. We talk about surprises and secrets in connection with the possibility of treats. In the course of happy parenthood we may overdo the finger-to-the-lips charade of 'Don't tell. Don't give it away. Promise?' on the occasion of, say, a hutch full of rabbits hidden in the garden shed ready for somebody's tenth birthday tomorrow. To an abused child secrets can have bad connotations, can create fear and hurt and apprehension. So don't go in, either, for dramatic wheedling and assumed cross expressions; they could strike too near the bone. Never, through the settling-in period, let a child who has been, or you suspect has been, sexually manipulated, become the focal point of a secret. Something being kept from him could mean that the cat's out of the bag and that the others are talking. Likewise, monitor the cuddles, terms of affection and endearment you use; keep on neutral ground until the newly-introduced child knows you well enough to disassociate your attentions from overtures.

So, explain insofar as you're able, each step of your family's actions. When it's a joke, spell it out. When your tongue's in your cheek, let the audience know. It can take a long time for a damaged child to shed his crushed emotions, and remember that before these are jettisoned he is unable, however hard we try to hurry the process, to let go of his past. He is probably confused about relationships which, in his former family, could have involved hurt and repulsed trust. No wary child can possibly know that he can put his faith in your ability to care for him without payment. Tread gently into his heart.

It is sadly true to say that the majority of fostered children would seem to be poorly motivated at school. However stable the placement or ostensibly happy the child, the attainment rarely measures up to the average. The good social worker can do her damnedest over the mechanics of care; the diligent foster parent can give attention and love and plenty of fish to stimulate the brain cells; the dedicated teacher can exercise patience beyond price and one-to-one help beyond the stretch of time, but in most cases to little academic avail.

I have with me a 12-year-old boy who is, by anybody's measure, an extremely intelligent child with a fine and critical mind. He stuns one with deep questions, uses a wide and adult vocabulary, can hold interesting discussions on God and the universe or the merits of sundry brands of potato crisps. He has the hands and untapped ability of a future draughtsman. Yet at his comprehensive school he commands a place in the special unit for the less able pupils. His grasp of mathematics is weak, his handwriting appalling and his ability to spell even simple everyday words very poor. (No, he is not dyslectic). His span of concentration is short; his attitude towards subjects, events and facts is based on a pick-it-up-put-it-down magpie pattern. The need to move about, to make a noise and put out feelers is too tempting for words. After the first nine years of his life at home in a fairly disturbed setting, he has now been living in the same foster home for the past three. He makes friends, is good at practically all sport, takes a keen interest in pop music and sees his parents regularly. He is mad about his looks. I have never seen him reading a book for pleasure; he is not anxious about doing his homework; he does not even sustain interest when, for instance, taken to a steam rally, circus or model railway exhibition.

I worry about his future, about the waste of potential, yet others tell me that, even with an innately clever child, his attitude could in the fostering situation be seen to be normal.

Then, on a different tack, one has the child from what is now referred to as a disadvantaged background; where education as such is not considered worth pursuing. The mind has been stimulated passively by dint of television and, often, by video films. Only the mental skills necessary for carrying on with everyday life are developed. Any desire for the acquisition of knowledge could be viewed with suspicion, or worse, with derision. A magazine is referred to as a book while a bound volume is, in many homes, not considered to amount to much.

A child coming into fostering from such a background experiences not only the grief of parting from his first family but also, even on moving into a moderately educated environment, a sort of culture-shock. He will be all at sea, more used to hearing arguments than rational discussions, struggling with a vocabulary new to him, ripe for the blanket of inferiority.

Here is a child who, already recognizing the gaps and never having been required to learn, will find schooling, and very likely in a new school, difficult and too much trouble. He, like the bright but disturbed boy, will be unwilling rather than unable to make the effort.

Every fostered child is living an unnatural lifestyle in that he is not with his own parents. He may not show any divergencies on the surface, but by the very nature of his case there must be occasional wonderings and speculations about past and future and the predicament of his present. His mind is less quiet than a 100% settled child; his self-image could be damaged. So he may resort to more blustering and bravado to cover the holes, or more hanging back like a shy violet, too nervous to squeak. There are, naturally, hundreds of fostered children who do not fall into either of these categories. Even so, tiny inroads of uncertainty must filter through. Parts which set the sights right and aim for the years ahead can go missing. Many would seem to opt for remaining inconspicuous in a crowd.

Foster parents must find time and patience to ease the child handicapped by his past, his disruptions, his inability to concentrate and his ineptitude for learning. An enormous amount of praise is due for spelling and so on, for the dreaded tables at last committed to memory, even for the days of the week sorted out in sequence. And do all you can to deflect comment and opinion from the brighter, perhaps younger and brighter, members of the family. Helpfulness is appreciated, indeed may be a lifeline for the little mind blundering through a fog; any hint of condescension is hurtful; ridicule and blame are not supportable.

CHAPTER 7

Hard to place

'Hard to place' is a terrible phrase when applied to human beings. They are those who have been displaced, by birth, rejection, abandonment, mental exhaustion, and fall like nestlings from some sort of an eyrie into an unwelcoming world where nobody may wish to pick them up. Many a baby is born straight into this bracket and is likely to be deprived of the instant initial mothering, warmth and instinctive knowledge that he is loved.

The infant whose physical handicap at birth has put his parents into a state of shock must wait in his helplessness for diagnosis and prognosis; he must wait for his parents' decision after they have discussed him, taken professional advice, weighed up his possible effect upon their family life now and in years to come. The distressed parents may come into the hospital's nursery to look at the child they have made; to feed him or change his nappy, to test themselves out on his incomplete limbs or exposed spinal cord or abnormally small head.

The majority of parents do decide to care for their mentally and/or physically handicapped children, even when there is no hope of recovery or repair. Others, who have reached their decision with equal anguish, know in their very core that they could not cope. One father of a child with pitiful abnormalities of the gut and bowel said, with love and grief but with relief at having made one of the most wrenching decisions of his life, 'we would have taken him home if we'd known it was just for a little while. We could have managed, forgive me, if we'd been able to see him with love to the end. Round-the-clock nursing, constant checking; almost certainly more operations, treatment, swings between hope and despair. Could we stand it? Working and looking after the other kids alongside his painstaking needs. I couldn't, just couldn't, let my wife do it. It'd kill her. You might rate me as a pig to ask someone else to foster him, but I couldn't face it. Nor has it been a flash decision to turn our backs. It's hurt us, almost driven us apart at times. Yet for us I know it's right. Whatever anybody says. We won't change our minds now. We value our marriage and the two healthy children we already have and, taking this little mite home, seeing him grow up with all those bags and things, it would break us in the end.'

This heart-rending account may be said to typify the kind of gruelling decision which leads to a family's child being left at a cross-roads. A long-term or permanent foster home is desirable, but will it materialize? The child may well stay in hospital for many months; he may be moved into institutional care; but, once the wheels of finding a home have been set in motion, efforts to find the right substitute family will continue; it may take years.

The fosterers of such a child must necessarily be drawn from that band of stayers who have both experience and a commitment stretching far into the future. Many foster children, it's true, touch upon the family very lightly and are gone. Even the healthy long-stayers eventually head for the world and simply become friends and contacts in the same way as one's own born children do. But the handicapped child, in all practical senses divided from the family of his birth, depends upon his second home and the people within it for all his early nurturing and often as his guarantee of a meaningful adulthood.

Prospective foster parents of the handicapped baby will be made fully conversant with his condition, its implications, the likely line of treatment and eventual outcome. They will in some cases have to prepare themselves for a child who, by the nature of his limitations, may not survive for long. Their constitution at the onset of caring must be metaphorically bull-like. These are parents who do not whine about getting tired or having had enough.

A foster mother writes, 'Shane was damaged by the whooping cough vaccine at the age of five months. His parents cared for him until the marriage broke and after a comparatively short spell at a home specially geared for handicapped children he came to us. He was almost three years old then, able to sit, but not to stand or walk. He was mainly bottle-fed, though he took a spoonful of solids reluctantly. He did not speak nor manage even rudimentary sign-language, but he had a variety of sounds which could fairly easily be picked out as happy, miserable, attention please! and no thanks, not by any amount of cajoling. I took to him at once. I can't explain why, but I knew he was for us. Not love exactly, not at first, but a sort of invisible drawing together, if you can understand what I mean. Both hubby and I felt it and knew we could take him. At fourteen years old he is not much further on in his milestones. He's tiny still and hasn't the strength to get on his feet, but he does get about on hands and knees. He's learned to drink from a feeding cup, which is more acceptable, somehow, than the old bottle and teat, and he can hold it himself too. He eats what we do. We prop him up at the table, just as we try in all ways to include him in family doings – and he uses a spoon very enthusiastically. An awful mess, but that's life, isn't it?'

This fostering couple has integrated Shane into a household which includes a grown-up working daughter and another normally developing foster son for whom they were already 'Mum and Dad' when Shane joined the family. There is no vestige of a chance that this boy will ever communicate verbally, become continent, form friendships in the accepted sense or participate in so much as a game of Snakes and Ladders. He will forever be a baby in all but size and looks. Yet that family loves him, tends his needs, includes him in all their trials and celebrations and treats him like a son of their own.

They face all the questions which impinge upon the parents of any growing child who will never be able to fend for himself. What happens when they can't care for him any longer, when they're old?

Then there are the multiples. Like the ready-made families up for adoption which feature in Chapter 12, the pairs, trios and quartets requiring even short-term foster care are also at a disadvantage. Some are not so bonded as to need each other's physical presence, thus you may sometimes be offered one or more of a complete set. However, more often siblings simultaneously taken into care do need the support of one another in order to survive their uprooting without unavoidable harm. Thus numbers of children related to each other are sometimes left in the limbo of a community home or assessment centre while fosterers are sought for them.

The first stumbling block is one of of accommodation; not enough room at the inn. There are limits to the number of children you can stand up in a modest semi. Then there is the undeniable fact that at least one of the bunch will probably bring problems with him. He could be a regular bedwetter; a monstrous thrower of tantrums especially in public; a chap with an aggressive chip on the shoulder; an irritatingly choosy feeder.

People are, correctly, prone to think extremely hard before saying a wholehearted 'yes' to taking on a young football team or part thereof. Settling in one child can be tough enough and so time-consuming that there are hardly enough hours for washing-up or having a bath or writing those urgent letters. It is a lot to ask; a monumental task to undertake.

Frequently finding a home for a ready-made family of children is helped along by advertising in local newspapers or broadcast on television by one of the home-finding schemes. In a few areas there are, literally, 'shops' set up to assist in the search for homes. This type of agency works with files and photographs in much the same way as an estate agent does on the housing front. But it works; finds contacts, gets a name for itself, catches open-hearted passers-by.

In spite of strenuous efforts, these little families of children could remain on the lists for a year or more. Sometimes the offer comes too late. The children have settled, made friends, have put down roots in their community home.

As with adoption, the older the child the harder to find him a foster home. By the end of his first decade he is already falling into the hard-to-place classification. The angelic hard-workers with exquisite manners and a terrific respect for their elders and betters will, in their minute numbers, take priority over the bruisers.

These half-grown children, whether fostered from the scene of their individual tragedy or by way of temporary care of Home, can be difficult to edge in. Coming at that relatively mature age into a second family is daunting for them, even frightening; shy- or bumptious-making – the reverse sides of the same coin. There will, more often than not, be a honeymoon period when they are too good for words; pyjamas folded like new-from-the-packet under the pillow; unsolicited help given with the drying-up; the cat treated to a catnip mouse from the Saturday money. We have ample time to tell the headmaster that the incoming boy is 'a perfectly normal little lad, no trouble at all all', and to promise the child a trip to the sea and the wildlife park when, alas, the honeymoon's over.

This feeling of the way is very usual, a sort of sussing out, of gathering strength. The child, when he has learned the ropes of the household, can begin to let reasonable proportions of his alter ego out for an airing. Thus, after a month or so of tranquil, helpful, well-mannered acceptance, the boy will, say, be hideously rude to you or pinch the cash from your Barnardo's box or take wicked pleasure in making the most stupendous belch at tea. Bravado-type behaviour of this kind is known in the trade as 'testing out'.

Testing out, in rarish cases, may not occur at all, or it may last a short and ghastly time, or it may gallop on into infinity without break. One of my testers, determined to see how far he could go and still be loved and wanted, set the house on fire. He staggered up the attic stairs with a can of petrol and started two prodigious fires fuelled with papers, clothing and surplus furniture. Thanks to vigilant neighbours, all lives were saved and the bulk of the house too. What was not saved was my affection for the lad; the testing out had continued for too long and developed too far beyond the danger zone. He got four years in youth custody: I got my second wind.

I do not wish to frighten prospective fosterers off this older child; the real unsettlers are not predominant. Remember, though, that you are accepting a young person with an informed opinion of the world he lives in and a clear determination about how he intends to conduct himself. Changes are only achieved by social and intellectual osmosis. Nothing can, with real effect, be forced. The child with a 'history', probably with a long series of placements behind him, can also prove hard to place. Some fosterers, myself included, like a challenge, though personally I prefer that presented by a small child with a hopeless prognosis rather than the repeater-firework type. The child with a whole lot of moves behind him can be quite a character, full of himself, cock of the roost. He wears people out, does schoolwork only if it interests him, makes and drops friends, borrows, and sometimes takes, what pleases him when it pleases him, sports his independence like a November rocket.

This type of child reaches breakdown mainly by his own almost willing instigation; he does not seem to want to remain in one place for long, nor belong to a mortal soul. He leaves, as in so many disruptions, an after-taste of guilt, failure, self-doubt and relief. He will stop at nothing until he has achieved his 'notice'.

I once knew a child who, placed with a family in the wake of his biddable half-sister, wished more than anything to move on. He deliberately killed the budgie, swore like a navvy, kicked in the cold frame and trod heavily all along the brittle rows of leeks. Still they loved him, strove for him, stupidly reassured him that he had found a home and would be their little boy. But he got them in the end.

He played upon the importance of his foster father's Sunday morning. This man, kindly and akin to all things natural, gardened like a being possessed in all available spare hours. Sunday mornings saw him up with the birds, scratching at the borders or heaving with the spade. Thus the good man rose at seven one autumn Sunday and, all the house sleeping, looked forward to an hour lifting the beetroot. Stepping into his wellies he recoiled sharply and was on the brink of being sick. Peter had done unmentionable matter in those boots. It finished him. He was taken back to base; and our family was the next.

Others who move on frequently fall into the category of teasers and players-up. The child who goes to a family where there are already other own/fostered children and who causes havoc among them can find himself ousted in order that those others may be spared contamination by him; the bad-apple-in-a-barrel syndrome. These types who are horrid to their peers, craving undivided attention, angling to get others into trouble, telling tales to beat MI5 are like earthmovers, heaving every muscle and using every wile to push the others out of favour. They thrive on surprise attack, even at the cost of subsequent security.

There will be a period, possibly quite a long one, over which the stalwart and dedicated foster parents will bend themselves into knots to tame the aggressor. There will be much talk between the social worker and the distraught foster mother. (Father's out at work of course and seldom, after vetting/selection/registration, sees the social worker at all.) But take heed; a repeater stands an almost

100 per cent chance of continuing to repeat. If or when such a placement collapses one is bound to ask why it was not foreseen and dealt with. Why was there no remedial action by way of counselling, the adolescent psychiatric unit, the educational psychologist, the professional assessors? In the meantime the hard-to-place become harder and harder to place. In the fostering world saints, willing to be battered mentally by a child whose problems prevent his willingness to conform to even minimum acceptability, are few and far between.

But it is true that while we generally get a chance to meet our prospective foster children and have time to think hard before we leap into another relationship it is also a fact that many of us, having worked miracles in the past, fancy ourselves as being able to work another one when actually our powers in that direction have run dry.

Teenagers, the largest group at any one time in need of foster families, are by definition difficult to transplant, difficult to change, if change be due. Adults who feel able to take on a child as part of the family and who hope for a real reciprocation of affection do not as a rule envisage this additional hand as being of riper years. Those who are stuck at home bringing up their own children, yet are at the same time drawn to expand their family, generally seek a foster child who would fit in and who is perhaps a year or two younger than their own offspring.

The average teenager is neither adult nor child but a mixture of both. Most teenagers think that they can save the world and quite a few know best. Quite a few more kick against all of what is known as authority. Some purport to hate their mother or father or both. Only a small fraction of those coming so late into care are adult or mature enough to see their predicament of needing a new family in its true light and with understanding.

'Beyond parental control' is a standard label slapped on to teenagers who are just that. This does not necessarily mean that they are beyond anybody's control, though it often does, which is why almost every county and borough tries its hardest to recruit professional foster carers for their teenage clientele.

These sturdy couples, and some singles, are put through a course of training to prepare themselves for all eventualities. These preparatory classes consist of discussions, lectures and, that bane of modern instruction, role play. They take place once a week, afternoon or evening, for a couple of months or more. Most areas still base this specialist teaching on the set studies, *Added to Adolescence*, introduced by sociology academics in America during the 1970s. Specific problems and situations are closely scrutinized with relevance to family mores in this country and such teaching is intended to help build the firm foundations on which succour and understanding of these incomers may be based.

Older handicapped children, possibly those who have become so through progression or acquisition of illness or those who are handicapped as the result of an accident or a non-accidental injury, suffer their rejection and the fact of coming into care loaded with a sort of double burden. Both age and disability are against them. Even as short a time as ten years ago, their chances, like those of the infants we discussed at the start of this chapter, lay more with the specialist institutions than with the private family. However, with today's imaginative advertising, the various agencies and contact groups which deal exclusively with hard-to-place children, even the teenagers with progressive disabilities can, and do, find a secure foster home for them.

CHAPTER 8

Private but not confidential

All through this book I've been sticking to the usual channels, the old familiars: the Authority, the Agency, the Department, the Social Worker, the Statutory Allowances, Sections 2 and 3, Court Orders and the 1980 Act. I, and those others who have managed to get a foot in the door of fostering, represent regular and registered parts of the British child care system. We are the *bona fides*, the ones who think our voices should be heard, who gather at the Foster Care Association's AGM, who muscle in on open evenings and generally think we know it all.

There exist, however, the private fosterers, who care for a quite different category of clientele. They make their own arrangements with the parents and organize the finances, the visits and the departures in their own style. These are the people who look after children who are not in care and where no recommendation, let alone an Order, has been made in respect of their immediate future. The only reason why the children do not remain with their rightful parents is that it is expedient for all concerned, with the possible exception of the children themselves, that they do not.

The need for private fostering is largely created by the demands of further education. Students, the majority of whom come from overseas, of all ages, cannot find enough good Christian homes open to their babies while they beaver away for their degrees and doctorates. The stress on Christian is of prime importance to many parents from the Caribbean and from Africa. There are dozens of advertisements in magazines and local newspapers crying out for such foster care.

Three or four years is the usual time sought for each placement; an eventual return to the first family is assured; visiting is likely to be regular but not frequent. If you wish to take on this kind of fostering and to advertise your willingness to do so, you are required by law to include your name and address in the advertisement. A mere telephone number will not do, while a box number is absolutely out. Furthermore, most editors require a covering note from either a doctor or a JP who is in a position to sanction your suitability. You also have a legal obligation to inform your local social services office of your intention to receive a foster child at least two weeks before that child is due to move in.

Expect, then, a friendly visit from a social worker and be prepared to give her all the details you have garnered on the case. Expect to provide her with your reasons for doing private fostering, to show her over your home, where she will pay special attention to the child's sleeping arrangements, proximity to loo and bathroom, and so on, and to answer a few personal questions without flinching. She will warn you of the pitfalls, and explain that you are not covered by the fail-safe legalities and undertakings provided for foster families registered officially by the council. She will also explain that the authority does have the legal right to refuse permission for private fostering, in the child's best interest. I have known only one couple to be refused permission to take a child privately on account of their unsuitability (a rocky marriage, substandard housekeeping, hostility to authority). If, however, you are given the green light, then you, like all other foster parents, must open doors to the health visitor when she calls, and to a representative from the social services as and when required. You will not have escaped supervision by deciding to go private.

One drawback to private fostering is the uncertainty of payment. Few students, or others who use this system of child care, are able to match the relative munificence of county and borough councils, nor to meet those extras I have talked about. Where the child is privately taken, out-of-pocket expenses are rarely recovered.

There is no scale by which to stipulate fees and no redress if they are not paid. I take one or two privately placed children from time to time and I make my own assessment of dues. I work out how much it is going to cost to feed and keep a particular child for a week (electricity, a proportion of rent/rates, toiletries, detergents, cleaning materials, motoring, special diet and so on), and multiply that figure by three. The figure you arrive at depends largely on your own standard of living and your own personal conception of what is necessary. The temperature at which you like to keep your rooms is a matter of choice, but it costs. Jersey cream on the porridge is a must at one family breakfast table, an outright luxury at another. If you're courageous enough ask for the maintenance to be paid weekly or monthly in advance it saves an awful lot of anxiety in both the short and the long run.

Scholastic agencies, who are listed in the London Yellow Pages, or individual schools and colleges quite often need fostering for overseas children from comparatively wealthy families during the holidays. A certain leaning toward gracious living is expected (your humble cottage home is not readily snapped up) and on-going interest and a caring attitude is assumed to be part of the deal throughout school terms. Most little eastern princes go home for the long summer vacation. Generous expenses are paid but there is no official wage as such.

Then there is respite care. This is a safety valve for long-term parents or long-term foster parents and comes both through local authority channels and privately. I have had children and young people from both sources. Handicapped in one way or another, these children put a tremendous strain on a parent and, however loving, that parent occasionally needs a rest. As fosterers we may become particularly adroit at coping with a certain type of handicap. I specialize, if that be the word, in short-term respite holidays for children with the rare Prader-Willi syndrome, a chromosomal misshape which affects muscle, growth, bone structure and intellect. Furthermore, it has a secondary disadvantage in that it leads to an insatiable appetite. These children must be watched the whole time, for they are on the look-out for anything edible. With their poor muscle tone and inability to take exercise, they acquire adipose tissue. The Prader-Willi person is full of charm, lovely to be with though given to occasional tantrums.

Foster parents with experience and understanding of certain physical and mental conditions and who are also happy to go private into respite care are like gold dust. If you want to take this on, a letter or telephone call to the relevant organizations within your area could start you off. MENCAP, MIND, the CF Society, the NSPCC, even the Salvation Army: all or any, in addition to social services, could provide the initial link between tired parents and willing foster parents.

Where your young guests are to be drawn from a narrow band, tell those organizations intimately concerned with such conditions that you are willing and able to help. Associations working on behalf of children with Down's Syndrome, spina bifida, cerebral palsy and multiple sclerosis may well be grateful for your offer. The majority of the specialist associations produce a magazine or some form of newsletter. Use it. The same rules apply. You must alert your local social services office a couple of weeks in advance of arrival.

Be realistic about your ability to undertake respite care. Don't be tempted to take on a child suffering from a condition about which you know little and have no practical experience. Be ready to learn and don't be afraid to ask questions before you commit yourself. We all have situations with which we can cope better than others and, equally, the reverse is true. For myself, I find that I am not as good with blind and blind/deaf children as I would like to be. I have not learned the way through darkness and silence and, much as I may want to help parents in need of both mental and physical rest, I am reluctant to subject their child to care that may be inadequate. Others among you may not be good with the mentally backward or, if you are delicate or frail, with the very awkward or the overweight. Recognize your weaknesses and concentrate on what you can really do well.

Private fostering may also involve the problems caused by differences of culture. If you have, say, a child of Ghanaian students, you have always to keep at the back of your mind a picture of the parents' lifestyle both in this country now and that of all the members of the family when they return together to their own country. Diet, manners, expectations and characteristics; find out where the child is heading, read about the country of his heritage, make friends of his parents, help him to straddle the gap between one culture and another. Do not offer him the soft option of becoming a little Englishman; he will not thank you later.

The area office to which a registered foster parent is affiliated occasionally receives requests from other parents whose children, though never likely to be taken into care, are nevertheless in need of temporary fostering for a specific reason. These freelance cases, where pressures are not too great, are often offered to registered foster parents. We are at liberty to take up or decline this extra work.

Most families seeking temporary care for a child are prepared to pay fees direct to the fosterer. Those who are not sufficiently well off are helped by the DHSS or the county itself. Reasons leading to once-only relief vary enormously: there may be sickness at home or the birth of another baby is impending. The impetuous flight of one parent, pursued at full tilt by the other, often means that another roof for a child must be found until connubial strife is calmed and home restored.

Women who run away with their children in order to escape from a belligerent man have been known, generally, alas, on a Friday afternoon, to turn up on the steps of the social services' office. Soft-hearted foster parents can usually be persuaded to take mother and her brood into their homes until things are straightened out on Monday morning. There is added spice afforded by the possibility of an inebriated husband or a wailing one beating at the door on a Sunday morning, or indeed the spine-chilling fear that it may occur; it depends on how you look at it.

Homelessness can also, from time to time, precipitate a whole family, temporarily, into a foster home. Of course we are at liberty to say 'no' when first approached, but, taken unawares and knowing there are four empty beds upstairs, it seems at the time so mean to refuse. But beware the pleading mother, toddler astride hip, who precedes her man with a request for shelter. One can prove an easy touch when caught in the role of a 'have' approached by a 'have not'. Twice have I been wheedled into taking in a little family *pro tem* when approached by mother alone, while her man sits low in the car down the street or remains at a safe distance while she does the talking.

These open-ended arrangements, though perhaps introduced by way of the social services, are not financed by them. Broadly, they are settled by private contract. It could be too late for refusal or withdrawal when the lesser half of this couple presents himself in broad daylight. They're in. The 'grass', the bottle, the lurching and incoherence do not constitute any excuse when pitted against the Housing Department's instruction to 'stay put at all costs'. Be warned: if you hold out your hand and are ready with temporary hospitality, you may just find it bitten off up to the shoulder-blade.

If you live a largish house and are known locally as a family who takes in children, then many variations on the theme are played upon your sympathies.

131

Apart from charlatans and fly-by-nights, our open door policy brings in many who remain lasting friends. Rachel, for instance. A London nanny, pregnant and on the brink of unemployment, she telephoned out of the blue at the suggestion of Gingerbread, the organization for single parents. We met, and within ten days she had moved in. I could offer warmth, food and company in exchange for her help with the foster children. She threw herself into our muddled and hectic life with verve, took Roy in particular to her overflowing heart, burgeoned with her own growing infant and, as the time became ripe, gave birth to a blonde and beautiful girl.

Rachel and her child stayed on with us, part of us, until she felt able to fend for herself again, to make a new life. Nannying is one of the few jobs where girls with babies are acceptable. I am happy to say that Rachel has never left us for long. Even today, with her bright star almost ten years old, she comes regularly to take over for a few days while I unwind, escape or otherwise make free with rare and unfilled time. I have known weekends when she has looked after as many as seven children with as little fuss as a mother rabbit. Loving and firm and unfailingly sensible, she has stood by us all with a very humbling gratitude for what might be termed the good turn afforded her over a decade ago.

Then there is Barry, a young man with a pretty unmentionable past who owes his honorary unification with our family to a tempestuous affair with one of my older fostered girls. Their first child, conceived beneath this roof, was welcomed by the pair of them. Barry lived on with us for a while, a rumpled young man in a room with Mickey Mouse wallpaper, mending our bicycles, drying our dishes and putting right yet another teenager who would not wash. He had an air of dash about him, drove a van and played football in the yard with the children. At midnight he would rush out for a Chinese take-away, share this feast in front of the kitchen fire with any who happened to be still up, and leave succulent pieces of pork in the foil dishes so the dog should have a treat in the morning. Sometimes he would return from dubious work with fresh trout and beg me to cook them very slowly in the oven. Always fun, always marvellous with the children, he too has never, in the wider sense, left us. Headstrong yet charming, quick to make retort yet deeply kind, tough as nails yet soft as an egg, within our family he has always been regarded as a sort of ebullient elder brother, one who lets the little ones sit astride his motorbike or hoot the horn. True, he occasionally gets caught with an offensive weapon or a roll of lead or a bloody fist; and pays the cost or does the time.

So the foster home, over years, expands of its own volition. Children who have grown up and left you may return for holidays and visits and, in the course of time, bring along their children. Parents of your current and past young things will call in and sometimes stay a day or two. Grandparents, younger by years than myself, will descend with chocolate drops, gloves they have knitted or biscuits for the dog. Boy-friends and girl-friends of teenagers will sit in the kitchen and brew coffee half the night, keeping the music low for fear of waking you. Your friend Lin with her hippy bus will turn up, filling the narrow road with her double-decker, your hearth with boots and infants. Folks who have been recommended to come and see you will unburden their poor hearts, dandle the children on their lonely knees, help scrape the potatoes, tack up a skirt or sew buttons on Ben's shirt.

Yet, for fosterers who are not all that taken with gregarious transgressors, those who cannot conform, and a house fit to burst, it is equally practicable and valuable to run a fairly tight-knit family home with a chain on the door and a mat with 'Welcome by Appointment' in the hall.

133

CHAPTER 9

Visitations

In a family of, say, six or seven children, the full-time-24-hours-a-day foster mother may well find herself dealing with as many social workers. The diary by the telephone is annotated with the linked names of child and relevant minder; the individual visits are logged. Calls, letters and telephone conversations punctuate the fostering year like so many standing orders, interrupting pleasures and chores alike and occasionally necessitating the hiring of a supplementary baby-sitter in order that full attention be given to a particularly knotty problem.

The sheer number of people involved might strike one as making heavy weather of what, to the inexperienced eye, appears a fragmented manner of tying up the statutory ends. Logic suggests that one good solid social worker, *au fait* with the foster home and constantly brought up to date on matters concerning the children there, could deal with them all in one albeit protracted swoop. But the system doesn't work that way, neither from the point of view of keeping the books straight nor in the interest of any particular child.

The world takes it for granted that, however loosely, each child not only belongs to at least one adult but is also cared for by one. The new foster parent, confronted by what she has, through preparatory study, previously understood only in theory, must come to grips with the reality. She must be ready to share a child's past, present and predictable future with the social worker. On occasion she must be gracious enough to take the back seat; to let the child ask advice or unburden his grievances privately to that social worker. This need to reserve a safe margin for child and confidante to communicate alone together upsets some first-time foster parents. They feel that, standing *in loco parentis* as they do, they have a right to be in on every last query, worry and uncertainty that the child harbours. This, as any experienced parent will vouch for, is far from the case.

Think back to your own childhood, and more particularly to your adolescence, if you can bear it, and remember how often you took your troubles to a person other than one of your own parents. An emotional bond, whether held by blood or by adoption, often actually precludes confidences of a more delicate or controversial nature. The child's reluctance to hurt you can run strongly (and you must be grateful for this consideration) and so render discussions on some subjects impossible. I know a boy who suffered being cold in bed for years because he couldn't bring himself to ask for another blanket; another who didn't care for chocolate but, because his new foster mother had opened a packet of chocolate digestives as a treat for his first tea, continued to eat similar treats with heroic tolerance throughout his stay with the family. So you must understand that your child's social worker, once accepted, becomes in many cases the buffer between a home which, however good, is a substitute for the natural home – and all the hiccups which disrupt the establishment simply by virtue of its being a foster home. So you must respect the privacy between the child and his social worker. Get up and leave them if you think fit after the usual discussion is over. Go and wash the coffee cups; take down the washing; play dominoes with one of the smaller ones. Get out of the way and let them talk between themselves.

Criticism on occasions there is bound to be. The many social workers who, over years, build up part of the fabric of our lives, come in coats of many colours. Some you will get on with; others make you feel so comfortable that you feel you've known and loved them all your life; some few irritate you or hold views so different from your own that any sort of meaningful rapport is impossible.

Sometimes we are over-sensitive about our conviction that we, in a lengthy placement, are the only people who really know a given child. We don't take days off or go home at five o'clock and sleep easy in our beds till cock-crow. There is never a vacuum, never more than a few consecutive hours without practical reminders of what parenthood involves. We are, if you like, mothers rather than women, and as such, are sharply aware and protective of our young. So it is good for us to be brought down to earth from time to time by the objective views of social workers.

True, we often see them as friends, and like it this way; yet we must never forget that they, unlike us, are, when they visit us, at work. The salient points of those visits are written up and filed, if not for posterity, at least for a good long while. We ourselves, our homes and our visible relatives are, even if ever so delicately, under scrutiny. We must be seen to be keeping our side of the bargain to ensure the optimum well-being of the child(ren).

Sticky times there will be. For myself, not over-en-amoured of the blood-tie cult, I have repeatedly seen the detrimental effect upon a child when an over-zealous social worker has re-kindled his interest in his natural home. The nervous little boy, low on self-confidence and what in the old days used to be called highly strung, is hyped up to make a visit home after almost a decade with protective and straight-laced foster parents. The dichoto-my between a rather right-wing and old-school-tie set of ethics in the foster home and the anarchistic ambience of the natural home, exacerbated by constant shuttling between the two, served only to turn the boy even more into his shell.

At the age of twelve this child is, frankly, confused. His loyalties are split and he tries like mad to brag about the bingo when doing a long haul in the foster home and similarly brag about, say, the Tate Gallery, when living it up with the natural parents. His foster mother, a wise old owl, sees the push for reunion as coming 'far, far too soon . . . a retrograde step as far as the child's road to a stable future is concerned'. She would have liked the occasional visits to her own home continued throughout the period of schooldays, and with the boy himself having much more say in the matter at around sixteen or so. 'When the damage is done, and yes, I do mean damage, we are stuck with it. Left to nurse along the lad with a limping leg in each camp.'

This fragile bridge between home and foster home can, unless expertly negotiated by social worker and proxy parents together, become the path to heartache, frustration and even anger.

Every child in care, whether fostered or placed in an institution, is allocated a social worker to oversee his needs – emotional, physical and material. Please understand that the foster parents themselves do not have social workers allotted to them; they are thrust upon them, one after another, as children with their various personal attendants come their way.

The child who entirely lacks any warm contact with, or, indeed, memory of a natural parent, and who has been shuttled between assessment centre, children's home, foster home and perhaps even a trial period with a welcoming relative, may see his social worker as the only stable being in his giddy life. When a more permanent placement materializes he could take a long time to accept with trust his new parents, so his relationship with his social worker is both strengthened and raised to prime importance. That man, or indeed more usually woman, might be the child's lifeline.

I have seen excitement fit to burst as we wait for 'my' social worker to drive into the yard. She could bring word from, or about, the first family; about the separated brothers and sisters; about the ideas for moving or for staying put. In a long-term placement she can cement the feeling of home, can put a seal of stability on what, in spite of all the foster parents' efforts, could have lacked that official assurance.

'She's nice,' offers Roy of his social worker, the fifth, alas, of his nine years in care. 'She's quite old and has got some children at home. At Easter she made us a cake with chickens on. She asks me about lessons and about the operation on my feet. I'm always polite to her and I get a feeling she likes me but I try to get away as soon as I've answered all the questions because I usually want to go out and play.'

Another boy, also aged ten, though far more mature in his perception, says, 'mine is always trying to get things out of me. Information about what happened when I was at my real home, but I never tell her the truth. I never shall. I'll keep them all guessing. I'd like to be left alone with my parents when they come here and she always turns up wherever we go. Once she pushed the door when there was something against it on the inside. She looks all very innocent but she's tough all right.'

Francesca, seventeen years old, is of the opinion that 'having a social worker is different now I'm in care. Last year when I was at home I didn't think the same as now. We were all brought up more or less to hate anyone who came in to interfere. I'd seen this woman with my Mum and had sworn at her many a time and told her to get the hell out. Now, though my foster mum is easy to talk to and really does understand, I like to meet my social worker sometimes during the lunch break from college. I can really discuss things with her – about my Dad and things like that. She's also very generous and is always asking if I need clothes or shoes and arranges for me to get special money for these. She helps me to get over to see my Mum and tells me all about what's happening at home but she also understands that I never want to go back there. Not while he's there anyway.'

Another teenager, just out of school and kicking hard against the world, driving his foster parents spare, drinking hard and in the habit of locking himself in his room, not unsurprisingly says, 'I've only seen the bloke face to face a couple of times. He can't do anything for me and I can't stand his oh-so-gentle bedside manner either. If I can't get out into the fields before he comes then I shut myself in. The last time he came he tried to get me to talk out of the window so I pissed in a pot and threw it over him. He needn't think I want any of that welfare rubbish.'

Tony, slow on the uptake by nature and not over-energetic, sees his social worker as the kingpin of existence, even though she has only had him on her caseload for the past six months. 'She's pretty. She takes me out sometimes and we go to the Little Chef for coffee and cake. She's arranging for me to go to some sort of centre to do woodwork and that. I'll have to wear the special overalls she's going to take me to buy. And boots with steel toecaps. She asks me if I'm happy but I'd never let on to her if I wasn't. They might change me to someone else if I caused her any trouble and I wouldn't want that. We all sit together, my foster parents and her and me and talk about things. She's a nice visitor to have.'

Of all these randomly chosen opinions, only the second and third children seem to have any real insight into the role which their social worker plays. Not even the older ones, on the brink of adulthood, seem to have any idea of the effort put in behind the scenes on their behalf; few would believe the sheer weight of numbers to each caseload. The ability of social workers to make individual children feel really special, however, does penetrate. One of the sad results of under-staffing on the one hand and the push for promotion on the other, is the rapid turnover of social workers in area offices. Children may barely become accustomed to one person and be willing to let their hair down when, for one of many reasons, they learn that their social worker is leaving. Pressure often leads to a less-than-perfect re-start, with notes scantily read and minor problems unnoticed within the shadow of more pertinent ones. Half a dozen such changes are not at all unusual over a long-term sojourn in care. This lack of continuity is not good but there is no way round it; it is an occupational as well as a situational hazard.

One must not lose sight of the fact that your foster child's natural family will often have a social worker, however remotely involved, of their own. In a little over half of all cases the same social worker will have to do with both parents and child(ren), but, if they live too far apart, then each may take his troubles to, and receive his balm from, separate sources.

Where a foster child has been placed many miles from his former home, and this can happen where there is difficulty in matching a child with special needs to a given family, it is often more convenient for the placing agency to delegate supervisory powers to a member of staff from the area office nearest to the host family. Under this arrangement a local social worker will make all the statutory visits and generally take over the ongoing welfare needs of the child. Any serious jolts such as change of school, gross misbehaviour over and above what might be seen as excusable, worrying medical or behavioural aberrations and the like, call for an on-site confabulation with both primary and secondary social workers. The annual review is similarly treated as an all-party affair.

One of the problems in placements of this kind is who picks up the pieces if things go wrong? This was illustrated in the case of a 15-year-old boy who, after almost a decade of recurring bouts of acting out, playing up and disrupting the peace, finally sought attention beyond his foster parents' ability to cope. Could or should a child like this be left any longer to amuse/disrupt/influence the younger members of the family?

So the fosterers threw in the towel; they were not legally bound to tolerate the unsupportable. But what of the social workers involved in the case? The original placing agency could well be excused a twinge of pique with their charge returning after so long and the virtual impossibility of finding a new place for a bolshy and obstreperous teenager. The local office which had also provided supervision over the years was justified in feeling it had been let down by the rejecting foster parents. The efforts to patch up, to come to terms, to persuade them to accept help and to provide counselling are all part of the hard-pressed social worker's burden.

There is a danger, when the pressure's on, of a certain lack of liaison between the natural parents' social worker and the child's ditto. This may cause troubles and misunderstandings and occasionally sheer bewilderment. Paula wasn't told that she had a baby brother at home until the infant was almost teething. The information had slipped the net. The parents hadn't written, because they couldn't, and the social worker thought she'd let the girl know, but hadn't.

Again, a boy who had much been looking forward to a visit home to his parents arrived there to find only chaos. The holiday should have been cancelled because of mother's depression and recent attempt at suicide. The message, conveyed from one area office to another and thence to the foster home, arrived after the child had set forth on this journey.

Occasional slips are only human. But foster parents, as rational beings, ought to be especially certain, in cases where two social workers are concerned with separate parts of the same family, to keep communications flowing. The social worker acting for each child is bound by regulations setting out the frequency of visits to assess health and happiness, progress and stability. These visits are set on a sliding scale according to variables of age, length of time boarded out, whether or not the foster parent is living alone or has a mate, and if there are any complaints, whether from a passing stranger, members of the household or, indeed, from you or the child.

A single foster parent must expect an initial check-up within the first two weeks of a placement. This probationary period is stretched to a month for a pair of foster parents. Thereafter you can expect a call, almost always by appointment, roughly every six weeks, or more often if you need/request it, until the child has been part of the family for a full two years. With the passing of those initial years, or the age of five, whichever is the sooner, the statutory visits take place at intervals of three months.

If you chance to move house, even so much as next door, your new abode must be approved and logged within the first four weeks of your move.

Any transitory placement (illness at home, new baby, pre-adoption or interim between the present and long-term home finding) likely to last less than two months must be followed up within the first fortnight, and again at intervals of not less than four weeks. This applies to all children of school age and below.

Those over sixteen who are placed on a temporary basis are seen by their social worker within the first month and then not necessarily again unless called in. More over sixteen who remain in care as the continuation of a long-term arrangement must be visited within three months of their birthday and thereafter when either summoned or inclined.

Every visit, in no matter which category and however uneventful, must be written up by the relevant caller and must touch upon the child's health, general well-being, behaviour and progress. Any other matters of substance, whether bouquets or brickbats, are also noted.

A parallel report on the state and condition of the foster home and the foster carers is also made and filed. Unless you are aware of a deterioration in your standards you have little to worry about. A happy home is not dependent upon the absence of cobwebs or the presence of cut flowers on the window sill. If initially your home was inviting enough to complement your willingness to become a foster parent, then the status quo will in all likelihood hold good.

No, what is far more important is your state of health, capability, emotional stability. If you are in any sort of a mess yourself this can and almost certainly will filter through to the trusting and dependent young. Some social workers are sympathetic enough to be taken into our confidence over our private problems and can smoothe our troubled waters with as much aplomb as our children's. Others do not, in manner or demeanour, widen their scope into counselling us. If you have personal worries feel your way delicately; get them sorted out in a way that is not connected with your fostering activities. Don't jeopardise the children's security because you can't cope with yourself.

The review is quite another kettle of fish from the humdrum report. It is a document prepared not only by the child's own social worker but together with a senior member of staff not generally personally involved with you or the child. A fresh eye, a new broom, call this what you will, but it does make sense. A tiny divergence from the norm, which both foster parent and regular social worker may have failed to notice over months, may be immediately picked up by a stranger.

I have a foster son, with me since the age of eighteen months who, at six years old, was found to be colour blind. He was not, as had been suggested, stubborn over certain learning schemes. Another had a marginal squint, barely noticeable except when sleepiness threatened to overwhelm him, which was similarly spotted by the outsider who came to monitor his review.

The first of these visits should be held within three months of placement, thereafter in theory, but to my certain knowledge not in practice, not less than once every six months. This recurring review must take into account any immediate or future deviations from the plans laid down.

Some, but not all, areas employ family aides who are helpers who move in on a daily or hourly basis to help mothers to improve their skills in caring for their house, home and children. This service, manned by patient and uncritical people, saves many a family from being split up by keeping children out of care. Many a time I have longed for a family aide, and I am sure many other fosterers do too.

We are, however, entitled to the services of a home help when weight of numbers or attention to a particularly demanding child leaves us short of time by anybody's standards. If, for example, baby twins were to be placed in family which already had children under a year old a home help would be allowed for one hour per evening to assist with bathing and putting to bed. Another example could be a summer holiday period covered by assistance for four hours a day, throughout which six children are amused, taken swimming and kept in relative order by a home help who happens to be a 19-year-old boy on vacation between one university term and the next. So when sheer collapse threatens and your mind reels under the strain of trying to fit forty hours' work into a 24-hour day, present yourself – haggard, drooping and heavy-lidded – at your area office. Plead for a home help, if only temporarily, to see you over a bad patch. And, for the sake of the children, you'll get one.

Some of us, but by no means all, get a link person, who provides a sort of giant shoulder on which we may lean or cry. She can also take our anger, our grievances and our occasional near-despair. When, as with our family, children are gathered up and brought together from an assortment of area offices, it is rarely possible for the composite domestic scene to be comprehended unless some quite extraneous person looks at the whole from the outside. So the link person is a sort of ombudswoman and if need be a fighter for change. She will both listen and act insofar as she can when confronted with a foster parent bedraggled by day-in-day-out caring and who hasn't been away from the children for, say, five, ten, more even, years; for it is one of the hard facts of lifetime fostering that one is deprived of freedom.

The link person will see what can be done about difficult children or those who for any other reason are particularly time-consuming. She might suggest visits to a therapist, remedial treatment, contacts away from the family so that the host family can take breather.

Health visitors; educational psychologists; peripatetic physiotherapists, infant teachers and teacher counsellors; graduates doing research on deprivation/transposition of maternal image/learning difficulties in fostered children/the Prader Willi syndrome/instinctive mothering, etc. Any or all in addition to your allotted social workers, and all who march in the rearguard of the social services, will drop in with or without notice. The interrupted day will be commonplace. Cakes and puddings will burn in the oven while immunization booster doses are discussed; saucepans will boil over like Vesuvius while the pros and cons of 'the Buzzer' are aired for a persistent enuretic; you will grab the mending box or beans to string in order not to waste time while obliged to answer umpteen questions from a list; your waiting bath water will cool to zero while a long story about certain unmentionable parents will cause you to yawn because you've heard it all before from the innocents themselves.

In the course of a year an absolute river of coffee will be brewed and swallowed. Many working lunches will be the forerunners of indigestion. Gifts will be presented when child or social worker goes to pastures new. Bartering will lighten the job; a couple of cabbages for a pound of lemon curd; a bag of gooseberries for ditto of blackcurrants; a copy of The Child Care Act, 1980 for a bit of help with composing a sonnet for the Regional Director's birthday.

There is a certain camaraderie between us all which makes for a very pleasant manner of carrying on.

CHAPTER 10

Burn-out

The breakdown of any fostering placement, even when measured against the tremendous relief of pressure which may have built up over several months, is inevitably flattening. You have admitted to irreparable failure and have requested the removal from your home of a human being who, compared with youself is at a disadvantage. Only under the direst circumstances could you cut off, for good and all, a child born into the family, or one who is adopted or with you under the umbrella of the new Custodianship: the child you have been fostering came without strings and with no obligation for you to soldier on regardless.

There was never any guarantee that that subdued 3-year-old whom you took in as a child of the family, and whom you agreed to bring up as such, would continue gentle and within the bounds.

Burgeoning security often brings out expressions of underlying anger, resentment and emotional confusion.

Does the kitten turn into a tiger-cat? And if so, why? For the insufficiently prepared foster parent, such a situation may result in exasperation which leads to rejection. Thus potential breakdown of care can be very largely minimized by sufficient training, by looking forward, by a knowledge of the probable. Increasingly, local authorities are recognizing that some type of provision must be made for training couples to acquire a real insight into fostering *as it is*.

The soft image must not smother the hard centre. Children are tough work in any circumstances, and when fostered

147

they are particularly susceptible to atmosphere, mood or anxiety. They do not necessarily develop any family loyalty. An enormous amount of tolerance, tempered by a firm head and hand, must override a temptation to make allowances or relax.

Of course no individual's prospective behaviour/inclinations/patience levels can be predicted to the last hair's-breath. However iron-clad we may be, we all have a breaking-point. The shocking fact is that approximately one in five of all foster placements do fail; most within the first to six to twelve months, some much later. This does not mean one in five foster children experience breakdown, for the majority of such breakdowns involve the same children over and over again. The real tearaways are difficult to contain and show scant regard for even the comparatively mild authority necessary to keep an ordinary family in trim. The severely handicapped of every kind can be so demanding of time and attention that even hardy carers may sometimes get to breaking-point through sheer exhaustion. Perhaps the unkindest cut of all involves the character clash which eventually has to be accepted as sheer incompatibility.

So much for the child's witting, or unwitting, side of family breakdown. Where, then, do the collapsing grown-ups fit in?

The answer can be broadly divided into two. There is the parents' inability, mentally and/or physically, to manage a given child and there is the destruction, or threat of destruction to the family directly attributable to a particular child's presence within it. No two children, or any of the diverse problems associated with any two children, are identical. The reactions of foster parents in the face of recalcitrant children are multitudinous. In some instances the attitudes of both parents coincide and can be worked through together. The sharing of these problems, even if total failure results, can make the event of parting less awful. The worst wrenches happen when each foster parent holds a divergent opinion about the child's difficulties.

Father cannot stand another moment of chaos: 'Either he goes or I go!' he screams, shaking an accusing finger at the child. Arguments can affect the whole family like a bout of 'flu. There are cases where children, whom the mother honestly believed she could bring round to normality by her stubborn perseverance, can, and do, wreck the marriage. The tragedy lies in rejecting a child in order to save a marriage. Tread carefully through this minefield when fostering a high-risk candidate; the merest tremor, felt at the wrong time, can explode a whole complex of hitherto firmly cemented ties.

Foster parents, after disruption, may feel that they have let the side down. They are devastated by the sense of failure. Some maintain that they can no longer live with themselves and are worried sick by re-examining past events. Yet we must understand that breakdown *will* occur, be it ever so seldom, throughout our fostering career. In our proud and self-centred moments we may see ourselves as saints, dispensers of tender loving care and in possession of rare insight. However we are in fact only a standard irregularly-shaped bag of protoplasm equipped with standard breaking points. It's hell to admit defeat and to have to make decisions which will hurt the least number of people the least severely, but in fostering it can happpen and, by the side of our necessary optimism, we must reserve a place for failure.

It is not all that rare for the child himself to engineer the breakdown, to ask for a change. This may come as a surprise where a sudden glimpse of the grass being greener elsewhere brings into the open subjects which have worried the child though been kept hidden. An unexpected burst of feeling could present the complacent foster mother with a basketful of home-truths fit to blow her into the horizontal.

I know a woman, full to overflowing with the milk of

human kindness, who, one seemingly tranquil evening, found herself on the receiving end of a set of virulent accusations. She was made aware of what her foster daughter felt about her. She was seen as being indifferent, as being a snob, as being in total ignorance of what children liked to eat. She could never quite come to terms with her madonna image again.

'That quiet girl,' she said, 'she whom I'd never once heard say so much as boo, she who sat at the dining-room table through six full months of meal times, tucking with gusto into macaroni cheese or fish pie and with whom I'd fondly imagined I'd established some sort of rapport . . . heavens, she went at me like a whirlwind, grabbed her coat, and was . . . gone!'

This lightning upset, striking when least suspected, can unhinge the most dedicated. In this particular instance the 15-year-old girl had, as she later divulged to her social worker, been biting back various little niggles about what might be termed etiquette for ages.

'O.K. then, so I'd been brought up by my Mum to say toilet and I still think that's the politest name for the bog. I mean, this is just an instance. But she called it the loo, which I happen to consider too-too for words. I knew it annoyed her, so I said it all the more. To make her rise I suppose. But she never did. And on that night I lost me rag one of the other kids was in the bog and she kept on about him being a long time in the loo, and I kept saying I was dying for the toilet. Then all of a sudden, like, I let her have it. Her awful milky puddings and all.'

We know it's notoriously difficult to absorb a fully-fledged teenager into the family, almost as difficult as it must be for that teenager to merge into your alien ways. Sometimes, indeed, giving up, magnanimously opting to present a chance to begin again somewhere else, may be seen as the obverse side of self-blame, soreness and the devastating sense of having avoided responsibility.

Teenage, even for children who sprang from our own

loins, can be hellish, both for them and for us. The fostered child, with the added burden of accumulated change, is even more likely to come a cropper, especially when resentment, the deep feeling of the world's uneven distribution of fairness, the thundering question of origin, come to be explored or understood. Even a child who has, since infancy, ostensibly been settled within a loving family, can rebel into explosion or resort to grey moods or demand myriad undemandables, when swimming into the middle 'teens.

Such a one, alas, was A. Always a loud child with a short fuse, he had been part of our large fostered family since the age of thirteen months. For many years he was the baby, the darling of his sisters, the charmer of all and sundry, good-looking and well-mannered despite the hyper-activity. School from the word go was fraught with complaints, veiled and otherwise. A's concentration span was minimal, his ability to keep silent limited and his interference with other pupils' working habits honed to perfection. Here was the 'acting' child, the surreptitious spoiler of other people's neat handwriting or lovely pictures, the disrupter of the class. There were those repeated occasions when he nipped off to the lavatories and failed to return to his desk which began to be looked upon as pluses rather than minuses-by-absence. Complaints in earnest began to filter home at the end of his first year's schooling and a request for his removal came at the age of seven.

The second half of his primary education was accomplished fitfully and with social and psychologically biased professionals in attendance. Academically A showed little inclination towards acquiring knowledge, nor did the imposed structure of the classroom rub off to any discernible extent.

At eleven this boy's IQ was judged to be above average, yet his attainment was already years behind, and his reputation as both evader and disrupter well established.

It was thought that his secondary education would be best dealt with in the somewhat stricter ambience of a boarding school where the influence of a house master and other male staff might prove influential over his somewhat wild demeanour. A himself was in favour of this plan, and it was decided that he should attend the same school as his older, adopted brother.

True, there were periods of rest between the eruptions, which varied in surface disturbance between niggling tremors and the mightiest forces of the Richter scale. Then, towards the close of his fourteenth year, concurrent with a phenomenal growth-spurt which took him to six foot four, A's behaviour took a more hostile turn. Bad language of the grosser variety entered his conversations with school masters; he was frequently insolent and he took to inflicting physical violence on boys smaller, though not necessarily younger, more frequently than is generally considered healthy.

So, from this untypical though by no means rare example of a difficult older child, the uninitiated may glean some idea of the delicately-balanced mixture of strength and patience needed to see such a job through without breakdown. By turns you are faced with a teenager who won't speak at all, who will use grunts as a means of communication, or who will assault the eardrums with almost unbearable vibrations. He is past-master at ignoring all words or advice, admonishment and love; he will drape himself about the kitchen watching you scrub the potatoes with a gimlet stare; he will be foul to visitors and wind up the younger members of the family. He will, in fact, impose his destructive forces as hard as he can – yet will be unable to present a reason for doing so or a goal he hopes to achieve.

Throughout this deadening phase which may last for months or years the dedicated and relatively common-sensical foster parent will be aware of the turmoil and hurt grinding about in the poor child's psyche beneath the layers of gloom. One of the toughest mental meals to digest is the fact that, the more some children lack love and sympathy, the ghastlier and more repellent their attitudes and behaviour. Those craving affection do their damnedest to repulse it. Human nature after all does have its breaking point. There are people otherwise good, kind and strong who crumble both mentally as well as physically when subjected to a sustained campaign of boorishness. If the other members of a family are on the receiving end of maternal failure then the disaster may turn to tragedy. Action has got be taken to minimize the upset to everyone within the family. Inevitably the axe must fall on the child who, for whatever reason has failed to respond to security, professional help, the patience of Job. If he cannot relax for any meaningful measure of time his insufferable behaviour, it is clear that it is he who causes the family's impending disintegration.

The breaking-point came to A, after long years of belonging to a family, when he was expelled from boarding school. His reputation for violence and lack of respect for authority proved his undoing. Once I realized that 'nothing we do, say or suggest makes any difference to him' and that our home was emotionally fragmenting in an atmosphere suffused with his sulky inertia, beaten, I threw in the towel.

Are we, then, what we are? Had I soldiered on would it have been worth it in the end? Could I, even by my own judgemental yardstick, be held responsible for letting an extremely angry young man loose on the world? Without a detailed follow-up answers to these questions must remain conjectural. We all know that rejection at any age leaves damaging scars; rejection at a growing-point when feelings are particularly sharp and self-oriented can really twist the knife, even when, by every gesture and utterance, that rejection has been self-generated.

Every foster parent must learn to relate to failure, whether resolved by the removal of the child or not, from a rational point of view. The good old British attitude of fortitude, of not letting the side down, rubbed in by a minimum of eleven years' schooling in the old mould and of centuries of doing our duty, tends to make us stick to a job long, long after the last shred of pleasure has dispersed. These are the conditions under which we feel that we cannot live with ourselves. Guilt displaces our reason. 'If I can't cope with this child, then who can?'. We are, presumably, the great unbeatable beaten.

In reality we are, of course, victims of clashes of character, of expected norms of behaviour, age, class and outlook or, and this is still largely unrecognized by the authorities for all its widespread occurrence, of pure and simple 'burn-out'.

Define burn-out, you say; explain the phenomenon. So imagine yourself at the end of that proverbial tether, having tried all remedies within your grasp, having given of yourself, your goods, your last thought and energy, until the thread which unites occasion to control finally breaks and it is impossible for you to do another stroke, cerebral or physical. The analogy with a battery is here ideally relevant; you have probably for years been giving with forbearance, understanding, incredulity, until one ostensibly ordinary day an infusion of child-related stress has a go at the last of the adrenalin . . . and it's all finished. There is, literally, no more to give. You cry that automatic, silent, movie variety of weeping which falls from the eye like quicksilver. You're done for.

This burn-out occurs more frequently in cases of single-parent fostering, where the mother (rarely father) has no emotional recharge save for that provided by the children themselves. Married foster parents, so long as their relationship with each other prospers and the work of the family is shared even to a small extent, less often reach this little-recognized low point.

The real pity of breakdown of placement through burn-out lies in the fact that it is avoidable. Foster parents, myself included, are not generally over-anxious to fall at the feet of the appropriate social services office at the first hint of strain. We are on the whole proud, and dislike whining when we ache a little. Yet it is tragically true that, even with the present-day pressures and resources, social service staff, on the whole, are inexcusably unsupportive about burn-out.

A really difficult child, one who must be watched constantly, who sleeps minimally, who creates noise fit to shatter a wine glass, seven days a week, and week after remorseless week, is the drip-on-a-stone syndrome that takes its toll on the carer(s). As a consequence, the rest of the family receives less than the best. Common-sense suggests a break; even a brief break. It's amazing how a couple of hours, say, free from the iron weight of responsibility, can prove restorative. Acting upon that common-sense, the backbone, after all, of the fostering situation, the fraught sufferer begs for respite. Could not the child who engenders the additional stress be diplomatically offered a little holiday, a weekend away, even a visit to an understanding and resilient couple who might stand in as an uncle and aunt? (People who are not up to the full commitment of caring are often willing to take an interest in a needy child.)

Yet we are told, almost as standard reaction, that homes have been closed in favour of more children being fostered; that places in those remaining homes cannot be found at the drop of a hat; that emergency placements must take precedence over casual or relief visits. We are told that it is hard to find couples who will remain steadfast in treating a child to days or weekends out. Indeed it is only recently, after almost 30 years of non-stop fostering and over the most monumentally difficult times that I have been offered a genuine and regular planned respite.

On the other hand, when absolutely up against the wall, say, when stress presses one to threaten the curtailment of a given placement, it has been known for funds to materialize so the troublemaker may take a commercially-run summer holiday with Camp Beaumont, Kids' Klub, or one of the growing number of similar, and very expensive, bodies which offer residential weeks. Generally speaking the fact that foster parents reach the point of total fatigue goes unrecognized. The local authority which provides, as a matter of right, relief care when the well of giving has run dry, will make social history. It will also save breakdown or disruption, as it is now officially called, heart-searching and, possibly, marriages.

One or two beds kept free for the exclusive use of children whose fosterers are weak with trying to keep their heads above the rising waters would not seem too much to suggest. An odd folding bed or two in a corner or two would involve no great extra cost; certainly minimal by comparison with the almighty sums spent in finding replacement families for boycotted children. The present shortsighted policy stands a local authority the chance of losing, for good, the services of parents who would, with a little nurturing over hard times, be able to soldier on usefully and lovingly for years to come. Waste, if you like, on two fronts.

Early warnings must always be acted upon within the family circle itself. Sometimes, even before placement has been agreed, a hint of disquiet over a certain child will ring small bells in a foster parent's head. Some among our kind can take up any waif in the world and make a place for him at table; most, however, and more especially any who share their home with spouse, grown or growing-up children and perhaps an existing fostered family too, have created a cocooned ambience into which certain types could not comfortably fit. The pernickety child, fussy with his food and unwilling to drag his heels through the stream or dig in the wild part of the garden for the skeleton of last year's interred guineapig, would be an uneasy member, both for him and for you, of any outward-bound sort of family which makes its own bread and encourages free expression.

You may imagine, given the stringent vetting you undergo, that an offer of seeming incompatibles would be out of the fostering question. But when emergencies arise any available port in a storm is approached. I do not suggest that you turn away all but the tailor-made; the port-in-a-storm situation is emotive, and we have all at times been pressed to take to our bosoms a desperate case, without question. Often these violent eruptions quieten as quickly as they blow up; the family drama is quelled, sparring parents mollified, displaced child reunited. At other times the emergency prolongs itself into a series of weeks, months, years. The matching may not even have been given a thought: a spare mattress was, at the time, the only consideration.

Thus the 3-year-old tyrant remains in the equivalent of a home for retired gentlefolk for longer than is good for anyone; the quaintly cuckoo 10-year-old flaunts his sore thumb in the face of academic excellence; the nubile school-leaver stays out ever later, much to the anxiety of her keepers, who long to go to bed at nine. They are all emergencies, but left where they were put only temporarily because nobody had the neck to complain. So, parents, remind your overworked social worker or whoever that the emergency is still with you. Either decide to come down on the side of keeping the bondable or start easing out the less adaptable visitor.

Many children who are fired precipitately into a family are in a roughly hard-to-place situation. The very speed of their removal from home and parent is enough to take the edge off the best of them. Others have been, and are still, the unwitting begetters of their own departure owing to aberrations in their own behaviour, whether imprinted or gathered up through close proximity to others with peculiar habits/ mannerisms/ outlooks/ beliefs. These, though regarded by social workers as requiring only a limited stay, fail to find either a satisfactory way back to the root family or, even by dint of much advertising, a new and permanent place in which to settle. The everlasting stalemate, at first so frustrating to the host family, gradually grows paler in importance as hope dies and the concept of there being no alternative to the status quo sinks in. Even in the case of an ostensibly healthy, happy, normally developing child, placed short-term while plans for adoption move snail-like towards a homely conclusion, the ultimate may never be achieved. Some young candidates, for all their own vivacity and sanity, cannot escape the threat to their own futures presented by parental failure. Such children, with the passage of enquiries, considerations and rejections, tend to cement themselves into the short-stay family and love grows. Thus we see that some children who, with their record, should have been delivered with an automatic breakdown factor built in can in fact, given time, turn the tables and flower in an increasingly secure state of permanency.

Foster parents who have experienced failure react according to temperament and in diverse ways. At the beginning we find the couple who, during the vetting, or even after the seal of approval which signifies registration, decide against fostering at all even before a first placement has been suggested. In many regions a preliminary course, either engendered by the authority itself, or following the guidelines of the NFCA syllabus, constitutes a compulsory forerunner of any first placement, but that in itself may still not be enough. The breakdown occurs in advance of the event; reality replaces theory; weaknesses which, for all the preparation, had remained hidden, suddenly manifest themselves. The ties, the strains, the negation of privacy which fostering would bring; these minuses weigh too heavily against the present and the benevolence sensibly fades. Possibly those who sweated over the preliminaries may be piqued but they also feel a parallel relief because withdrawal has been thought through. Nothing has been lost but time and face.

Most newcomers, freshly-registered and bursting with confidence, sweep into the initial placement with verve. The children, however, may fall within that difficult bracket that includes a non-sleeper, a gross fidget, a 24-hour fog-horn, a type who throws up any meal. Then there is the desperate toddler who refuses comfort, who cannot even minimally understand his uprooting, who pines and whines in spite of every last effort to provide a cushion of love and safety. Such a child can ruin good intentions, however firm and however readily accepted by the social services panel hungry for homes. A bad start such as this can undermine resolve and confidence. The little quiver of failure grows into a sort of fear of repetition which concludes the exercise into philanthropy. Never again, they say as they resume sleep-filled nights, tranquil days and freedom to serve Madras curries or tripe and onions as they fancy. Their fostering days are over.

More's the pity. Had they experienced an easy child initially, the slow building of wisdom would have eventually equipped them with the ability to cope with almost any type of small human.

At the back of the fosterers' minds, then, there is always the reassurance of the knowledge that by right any placement may be terminated at pretty well any time, and on demand. It is an overwhelming realization, particularly when the temptation to give up runs strongly, which has a frightening, power-from-on-high quality. It must never be undertaken lightly, never used without the solidest of reasons. Yet, just sometimes, to ignore that right because of a stubborn determination to see the problem through could be a less wise decision than to admit defeat.

A family, years after taking on a small and recurringly troublesome primary school girl, brought themselves to beg the social services to find her another place, after they had put up with great spans of rudeness, temper and non-cooperation. They had tried to make the girl fit in; to exude a kind of ectoplasm proffering security. The gulf which had been apparent from the beginning never really closed; the sense of independence in the child clashed with the will of the foster parents to provide a mental and physical environment governed by what they described as encompassing love. When, at the age of sixteen, the girl was given her freedom, she felt rewarded by her patient non-giving. The foster parents, on the other hand, came off less well; ashamed of their own relief, they felt unable to consider another placement, saw themselves as being predisposed to failure. Breakdown had broken them down – after an eight-year marathon.

Undoubtedly bad matching has much to contribute to disintegration; the fighting of differing temperaments can only intensify as, say, when the wilful child grows older and wordly-wiser within his equable foster family. Odd phases of peace and true affection interreact with outbursts of fury and animal frustration. Parents can actually become frightened by a forceful adolescent, would give anything to see him safely ensconced in someone else's sitting-room.

It is improper to expect gratitude from a fostered child. We know that his predicament is seldom his own fault. The commiseration of friends and neighbours who, following his ignominious departure, throw cold water onto the already cooling ashes of the heart by saying, 'and not a breath of thanks after all these years!', 'after bringing him up from so-high!' and 'I think you've been wonderful to stand it!' only cement the rejector's dejection.

Breakdown, by the nature of our human condition and the vagaries of our myriad constitutions, is almost bound to crop up within a full fostering life. It is often necessary to liberate both the child and ourselves. We must be big enough to recognize it as change, not as failure.

CHAPTER 11

Enough to make you sing

Thinking back over the midnights through which this manuscript has been written I detect a certain weight. Yet I am up to my neck in fostering and have been for jolly nearly three decades. So why, stabbing into the loose pages as if to catch a flaw by surprise, do I find so much adverse propaganda, so many warnings, so deep an urge to turn people away? For, when airily off guard I throw my invisible hat into the upper atmosphere and turn hugely euphoric about the sustained joys which, overall, permeate this lifestyle.

I have harped on the difficulties and the harsh and think-again problems because it is important to me that those who might not make a good job of other people's children are dissuaded or prevented from doing so. I feel protective: I would like to ensure that sharp little infant edges are smoothed by hands which deserve them. So many children, even (perhaps especially) those who wear the exterior of an armadillo, are broken and in disarray within: I am fearful lest they be misunderstood by the tidy-minded.

I must therefore make redress for my constant complaints over the misjudgements of social workers, the tediousness of in-depth vetting, the destruction accomplished in a day's work by recalcitrant teenagers, the awfulness of the outright rude and unsociable. I have absolutely no doubt whatever that the everyday good things, even if submerged beneath neglected homework, lost gym shoes or a truly terrible mess to clear up in the bathroom, really do win hands down. Today, for instance, with our numbers reduced to five because Tom has been invited out for the weekend, we are all able to fit into the car without fear of being apprehended. We consult together over our Saturday breakfast of boiled eggs and decide upon the country park. The picnic we prepare is prodigious: pink salmon and bananas, sliced wholemeal bread and Bourbon biscuits, Battenberg cake and roast chicken, some cold bread sauce for Ben and half a cauliflower. The September sun shines bright and yellow; we play I-spy in the car; nobody is sick; the man on the gate lets us in at a very slightly cheaper rate because our new child is so small for five. The pygmy goats let us stroke them; the rabbits mate before our eyes; there is a whole phalanx of swings; a trampoline; an assault course; a shop which sells plastic snakes and very expensive home-made lollipops.

You can print your own keepsake; go up the giddy spiral staircase of a folly; stretch your intellect by paying attention to an exhibition of sheep-keeping in the nineteenth century and/or one on William Morris, his prints and papers. We push Ben in his wheelchair up three-in-one banks, admire pens of bantams, catch sight of a stag with two does and are regularly required to find, urgently, bushes for one hopping child or another.

Tea out includes all those treats assiduously avoided by the health-conscious: chips and turkey-burgers (turkey-burglars) and garlic bread dripping with cholesterol; fizzy drinks (two out of five spilled on the table) loaded with EEC additives; and a stick of caries-inducing rock apiece to chew and spread over the car seat on the way home. With autumn making strong hints from the beeches, it's been a lovely, totally child-orientated step on the way towards chillier days and darker nights. In no way do I regret whole slabs of time consuming my total attention and spent entirely with and for these five miscellaneous young. The full-time foster parent is not just doing good, or being a do-gooder, but is, most of the time, getting as much as she's giving.

There is a strong trend nowadays towards standardizing and, to some extent, professionalizing fostering. It is, in some militant quarters, considered to be grabsome, sloppy and treading on the natural parents' prerogative to want to be called a foster *mother*. Foster *carer* they like. Given time, will the foster *keeper* stride over the horizon with her credentials tucked under her arm?

When considering the plight of children in voluntary or Section 2 care, then perhaps some of the terminology and what lies behind it needs to be thought about by the maternals among us. In many cases these children will be returning to their first homes within weeks, months, years. Of course we must not presume to take over or play down the importance of those real parents. I have yet to meet any foster parent who insists upon being known as Mummy or Daddy while there is so much as a glimmer of interest in or contact with the original(s). In practice, however, I have found throughout the long years that most children staying beyond a very temporary spell do slide into the familiar; one becomes Mummy almost without noticing. Yet this promotion has nothing at all to do with the displacement of the natural parent. Even children of three and four make an instinctive differentation between the birth mother and the foster mother.

All children, in order to function wholly, need a central figure to their lives, a figure who provides warmth of three distinct kinds: the basic comestibles, joy, and an innate ability to understand. In the absence, for whatever reason, of a young child's first mother, a substitute must take over those essential stabilizers. He cannot be left in limbo, grieving without comprehension, aching for his creature comforts, without sustaining damage. We have all seen the terrible void, the numbed sensitivities, the inertia or the obsessive habits of the child who, as an infant, was not cuddled. The cot-nursed baby, the one lame dove who was ignored among a clutch of older brothers and sisters, even the infant brought up on a very strict schedule can stand still on the emotional level until such primary necessities have been met.

The foster mother, whatever the child or the avant garde or the rigid preserver of rights terms her, can and does provide such physical and psychological nestling. With fortune on his side the child may return to his natural parent and the process of growth will be able to continue in line with a good and average pattern.

Mother-love, whether engendered by a real parent or a substitute, comes free. Feeding, clothing, stimulating and educating a child do not. Traditionally fosterers have been paid enough to cover those outgoings directly connected with raising a child efficiently. In the past, and the relatively recent past at that, this allowance was little short of invisible, a real cheese-paring. Now, with a realistic estimate of costs, foster parents receive enough (with access to additional special needs) by any average standard. Yet the new wave of carers, to my knowledge in at least one borough, has actually set up what would seem to be a kind of strike over payments. Foster parents were for a period advised to refuse to take on any new children unless they were paid twice the previously accepted rate and a small wage.

Indeed, the Charter adopted by the National Foster Care Association as we have seen includes a resolution that 'carers be given the opportunity to receive payment for their time, energy and skills'. For this to come about, and I don't see why it shouldn't be practicable, there could be a two-tier option. We could stick to our old-style system of maintenance plus extra money for any real needs, with parenting coming in for free. Alternatively fostering could be a job, like any other, for which payment was made with additional allowances for specific expenses related to child care. The two bands would have to be treated differently for insurance and employment benefits purposes, but this could well become the pattern of the future. You may be able to choose; foster as an extension of the family circle or as work?

I pick a ticket from the bag in order to find another day which made the heart glad, pay or no. The little boy, a town boy, very down-at-heel, was with us for a month while his mother both received treatment and gained a modicum of time to recover from strain, struggle and breakdown. Harry, one of the born-to-fail brigade, carried the cares of his own world on his bird-bone shoulders; his mother's debts, the attitudes of his schoolfellows and teachers in respect of clothing, language and aroma. Adult company and conversation had aged him miles beyond his nine years. There was nothing concerning certain insalubrious subjects that he did not know. In stature he was tiny, elflike and brittle. Academically he had not even begun; he could not write his name, draw so much as a stick-man or read a sign saying 'Stop'. He would break his fairly strict dietary preferences to eat bread (without butter or marge, but with red, only red, jam) and chips with plenty of vinegar or brown sauce. He would drink Coke or, second best, fizzy lemonade. Water, he maintained, 'turned 'is stomick'.

We took Harry to the wildlife park. One of a party of six or seven children, he nevertheless hung back with me, reluctant to let off steam or run with the herd. His falsetto squeaked apprehensively; he 'didn't loike no animals 'cept p'raps efflants' and would prefer to stick to the paths. He looked to neither left nor right, ignoring the great aviary of vultures as he quizzed me earnestly about the entrance fee. Why, he wanted to know, had I 'split' on Ben? Ben, too, was small for his age, nothing like five; and those iron things on his legs, Harry assured me, would have got him in scot-free. My Anglo-Catholic girlhood rose from the subconscious like a helium-filled balloon; a homily on the subject of truth and conscience bubbled up just about as far as my larynx before, quelled by Harry's assurance that I could cut corners if I tried, I had second thoughts.

'I'll try it next time,' I promised, fingers crossed for a lie. As this particular park did not aspire to elephants, I lit upon the idea of the rhinoceros enclosure as next best thing. Harry had not yet deigned to lift his eyes to meet those of a single beast, even after my happy information-laden chat and that of the wildlife-mad children. Covered in rich grey clay, the rhinoceros family (all three) was out on the grass, ponderous as the Ice Age, swinging their heads from side to side as though possessed of inbuilt metal detectors. Naturally they ignored us. Harry ignored them.

'Can't smell no smell,' he remarked, his glance on his sandals, and we moved on.

I tried the Children's Corner, took him to the rabbits with lop ears, the carrot-coloured guinea pigs which he would have been allowed to pick up and the simply enormous striped pig. The rich fragrance from the sty excited him; the first flicker of interest came into his pinched little face as he caught sight of the swinging underbelly of the vast sow.

'Cor blimey! See 'er tits!' he squeaked, rousing by-standers and causing the embarrassed animal to mince off on her neat trotters to the decent shelter of her sty.

The pony ride was not nearly as successful as the pig. Harry allowed himself to be upped into the saddle without protest, but also without changing his vacant expression. The reluctant, bored pony progressed from the standstill, the child swaying and clutching the reins to the pommel; a twin picture of unwilling beast and unwilling rider. At the end of the affair Harry waited, motionless, to be taken down, took my hand gratefully and said, 'Well then, that's done with.' And I explained to him that, if ever in a similar predicament, he must say he'd rather not have a go; that I would understand.

'You bought all them tickets for the 'orses,' he answered, 'so it weren't right, were it, for the money to go to waste?'

We had tea in the ritzy restaurant where he tucked in as though sponge fondants might fly from his hand should he let his eyes stray. He chatted away to the others, insisting that the efflants were best, making them all giggle and lose control of their swallowing. It pleased me to see my regular children putting themselves out for him for they had, I'm ashamed to relate, not treated him as kindly as I would have liked. His babyishness and quaintness had not appealed to them and, after a few false starts, he had been largely left out of their games. Thus he had become mine for the duration.

Now, kicking his feet against the table in the tea-room, he played the fool and became one of the gang for a while. I watched him stow a cake up his jersey, a little etcetera against hard times, and said nothing. Then the others left Ben and me and ran to the giddy delights at the park's adventure playground; a Trojan horse with trapdoor to disgorge small boys, a narrow plank two feet from the earth along which to teeter, a high and mighty helter-skelter, a sandpit like a small Sahara.

Harry, however, hung back from such childish adventures, watching. From time to time, on the move, he inspected the constructions, gingerly touching wooden struts, rubber motor tyres, ropes and cold tubular bars. Once, off-guard, he allowed himself to play for perhaps five minutes in the sandpit; he trickled the ochre grains through his fingers, scoured out a road, drove a fir cone down it, had an almighty crash with an old yogurt pot and yelled momentarily with heady glee. Then, as if disapproving of his own pleasure, he straightaway withdrew to the bench where Ben and I sat, and wished to forget, or so I imagined, his brief regression into the world of pleasure.

167

Going home in the crowded car he disregarded the minor squabbles all round him and, oblivious, sank into sleep. When we arrived back, he did not fight, as the rest did, against bed. As he slid again into sleep, I tucked him in and said we'd had a nice day, hadn't we? And from some distant land he brought back his grin and said, 'It were the most best day of me loife, honest. And them efflants was so big . . .' In his hand, folded up close to his right ear, he clutched a mess of fondant icing and squashed sponge cake. A crystalized violet stuck to his lobe like a girl's ear-ring. I picked up a somewhat sticky jersey from the bedroom floor and took it down to the washing machine. Dear Harry.

I know I've already given a deal of space in the context of really quite severely incapacitated children, to the fors and againsts of what used to be called institutional care, and which is now generally termed residential care as though fostering *per se* might not be. Most of us who foster will be asked, at one time or another, if we would be willing to consider taking such a child, even though this may be for as short a term as a relief weekend. With the acknowledged approval of all who work with and for the handicapped it is open policy to go for family-orientated care, yet there is a shortage of individuals who feel able to make a long-term commitment, particularly on account of an older and probably institutionalized child.

Successes (and this chapter is meant to be concerned with the plus side, the successes) need not be measured in whole figures, nor in the giving of promises to be held for years and years ahead. I will tell you about Kevin.

He was already twelve years old when I was asked if it were possible for him to come to us. By this time he was at school, one exclusively for children with cerebral palsy, but he needed a family for holiday periods and to take him out for the odd days here and there during the bits between. This boy was not as badly affected as many spastic children; he had a very adequate vocabulary, though could be hard to understand sometimes. He was mobile, even without sticks, though his legs tended to run away with him if he tried to go too fast. He got on with people, was invariably polite, though he made a nuisance of himself by not letting go once he'd buttonholed a listener.

This last point, common to institutionalized children of almost any age, is one of the first and most noticeable signs of having become thus affected. Other habits acquired are an incomprehension of the needs and wishes of other people; compulsive eating for comfort, excessive choosiness over food; there is also a high expectation of organization as a matter of course, including treats, outings and entertainments as well as the practical daily round of lessons, meals, recreation and so on. In short, the institutionalized child avoids decision-making yet creates pressure by his demands. Kevin was such a one.

Like many a naive visitor, I was struck by the boy's overt friendliness, his forthright and happy manner, his apparent wish to latch on. Flattery perhaps? Anyway, on the strength of that first meeting our co-existence for a considerable slice of the future was sparked off. Kevin became, albeit as a part-timer, one of us.

Having never for so much as a day lived as part of a family before, things rather went to his head. It must have been like a ticket to some boundless country, a place where free time had somehow to be dealt with and, like it or not, adults were not on duty in the formerly accepted sense. He took, in fact, to hanging around me, asking what he could do next. I gave in to the extent of letting him help with almost anything I was doing, be it tidying the beds, making a bread-and-butter-pudding or mucking out the goats. His endless chatter wore me down but, fool that I was, I kept on mothering him instead of letting him out on a short leash towards independent action. At the age of twelve, I could hardly expect him to go to bed with the little ones, so the stream of sometimes incoherent words and intermittent demands for milk shake, slices of toast, shoe-laces to be tied, stories to be read and early social history to be listened to, rendered me impatient. With not a little regret I realized that Kevin was governing me.

As soon as I had taken this on board I began to mend my ways in order to improve his. His handicap could not – must not – be made an excuse for pity. The way he was behaving was appalling; things had to be done his way; his voice had to be heard high above those of the other children's; the last piece of cake, the last biscuit, the last sweet, all were automatically regarded as his; sharing had not been invented nor had other folk's reactions been deemed worthy of notice.

I began this rehabilitation, or imprint-changing, by giving him the chickens to feed, the dinner table to set (good for hand-to-eye co-ordination, this) and the cutlery to put away into the basket. It was simply taken for granted that he would carry out these jobs for the good of the family, just as the other children undertook their special tasks.

Reprimands were based on the do-as-you-would-be-done-by system, a system I try to operate with all my young. So if the chickens were still queuing up for grain and withholding their eggs at 11 am, while our own elevenses lay temptingly upon the kitchen table, I would muster all my strength to say, 'Kevin, I'm sorry, I don't wish to be mean but if you can't be bothered to feed the hens, who are decent enough to give you eggs for breakfast, do you think, honestly, that you deserve buns and coffee this morning?'

Similarly, the dinner would be kept waiting if he forgot the table. And very gradually he learned to work with us, as part of a private team functioning without the help of a verbal or written time-table, responsible for helping our own world to go round.

By giving him affection and trust and a firm push to get on with it to the best of his ability, we also gave him a pride in the tasks he undertook. He grew accustomed to no longer being waited on, he learned to tie his own laces, to use a pair of scissors, to aim straight in the lavatory. Socially he was beginning to shape up. But after all those years in residential care he could not accustom himself to household shopping, to situations where we ran out of things, or to even the smallest scale finance. He had, of course, been used to spending his pocket money on sweets and fizz and cards and the odd stamp, but to be asked for little packets of Bisto or custard powder threw him. It could, he maintained stubbornly, be sent down automatically. Indeed, he imagined that if any domestic gadget or piece of furniture wore out or was damaged, all that was necessary was to put in for a replacement.

I remember his cold-comforting words one evening when, after the smaller children were in bed, we knelt in the decidedly chilly sitting-room attempting to make the firewood catch in the grate. The kindling was not dry and the matches died one after another. Kevin was by this time about fifteen and pretty sensible in many ways. He had recently undergone an operation to make his gait easier. But he still had this absolute block about money.

'Why don't you put in for central heating?' he asked with real concern. 'They never should have left you this long without. It's not good enough.'

'Who's *they*?' I replied.

'The government.'

At seventeen Kevin decided, of his own volition, to opt for a young men's hostel, a sheltered house for the handicapped where individuality was encouraged and from where he could travel daily to a special workshop. In hindsight I can be almost 100% certain that this regression to residential accommodation was triggered off by his search for security. We, with our precarious way of living and our piecemeal finances, had never really taken the place of the solid strength of his institutional rearing.

He never answered our letters nor in any way contacted us any more, yet I do not look upon his five years with our family as wasted. I am confident that we all, not least Kevin himself, worked to change a self-centred little boy into a reliable and thoroughly likeable young man. And that's enough to make you sing.

CHAPTER 12

Fostering – back door to adoption?

Can fostering provide a circuitous route to adoption? A live thread of possibility for couples (or singles) who desperately seek a child of their own? A thoroughly legal member of the family, a child whose welfare, happiness and future is inextricably bound up with the whole? One who is open to real recognition by grandparents and other relatives, a knot which is never unravelled even with a long-term fostered child?

Well yes, fostering can perfectly legally be used as a stepping-stone to adoption.

We all know that real adoptable babies, blemish-free and of healthy pedigree, are rare as gold dust. Whereas in the (good or bad) old days infants new-born and hungry for homes were placed in their thousands with ideal couples, today these placements have fallen to a trickle. Prospective parents must meet every last and stringent statutory requirement. The vast majority are under thirty-five, are securely employed, without financial or domestic problems, well housed, happily married to one another and more than ready to give time, love and unlimited consideration to their special baby. They have paid dearly in terms of gruelling investigation for their child. They have answered questions which might have turned lesser people scarlet; they have probably had to wait far longer than any fertile couple's nine months. Yet, however hard the going, however protracted the pseudo-gestation, the exercise has paid off in the end. The child, weeks old, night-crying, colicky, seeming in need of constant attention at one end or the other, is theirs. Though let's concede that he does gurgle too, does kick in the bath, does give a wobbly smile and does wave his hands about as though communicating by semaphore: all those lovelinesses as well.

We are not, in this book, concerned with such comparatively trouble-free placements.

Our concern is with the single woman, the single man, though he is rare, the married-late couple, the unmarried couple, the firmly welded couple who discovered their infertility too late to qualify as suitable for adopting. Consider too the couple who started on the baby list genuinely but became frustrated or fed up with the long wait. Add to the adoption scene those who want to enlarge their existing family but prefer not to create any more children of their own; call them the altruistic adopters if you like.

Children are frequently advertised, nationally and locally, as being in need of fostering with subsequent adoption a possibility. Others, having been placed with foster parents in the normal way, afterwards become free for adoption and made available to those parents; a move up the security ladder from the leasehold of fostering to the freehold of adoption.

Very occasionally we, the fosterers, decide against the proffered adoption. I have done so myself in the case of a hard-to-place infant who had seemed so safe and sound and insulated against any chance of rehabilitation. Would I, I was asked, consider taking on the legal parenthood of this baby who, in the absence of any interest shown by natural relatives, would require long-term care and a lifelong family?

As a single woman, divorced long since, and with a couple of adopted children mingled in with several of my own and several fostered, I considered my bank balance before the equilibrium of my heart. No, I said, I could not afford to take on the financial responsibility of another child; it would not be fair. He was, in any case, a perfectly 'safe' boy, well established within our family and with parental rights vested with the local authority. I would rather keep on with the straight fostering arrangement, maintenance and all, and keep our heads above the water.

But, alas, I had not taken into consideration the vagaries of consanguinity. Fourteen years on from that day when the tiny boy had been collected (nappiless, we discovered on the way home in the train) from his municipal nursery, and almost certainly as a consequence of the then-new and somewhat militant views on ethnic matching in fostering, his first family, with half-siblings born subsequent to his placement, expressed a wish to meet their son.

My complacency had been misjudged. Had I taken the opportunity to adopt during the heydays when love, security and happy family life were deemed more important than pigmental tallying, then none of this later shunting about would have been legally permissible. There is nothing to prevent a parent or child discovering original roots after the age of eighteen, but by almost any standards an unveiling of primal relationships during the early and middle teens in a heretofore stable child can create an emotional rumpus of the most disturbing variety. I had, then, let my chance to cement that child's place in our family slip by, and have lived to regret it both for him and for us. Possibly for his parents too.

Let's look at some veiled adopt-a-child advertisements. Nine-year-old John has 'blossomed since coming into care nine months ago. He has become talkative and full of questions and enjoys someone reading to him. He is proud of his clothes and takes particular interest in his appearance. An adoptive home is urgently sought, with ongoing contact with three brothers aged 6, 5 and 3'.

John's siblings are also on the look-out. 'David (6), formerly hyperactive, has calmed down a good deal. He takes an interest in his surroundings and loves cuddles. His behaviour matches that of a 4-year-old and academically he has achieved little.'

And 'Fred is an appealing child of 5, though inclined to be critical. He is behind in development of speech and may not be very bright. He has a minor congenital heart defect and will require dental treatment.'

For the purpose of example, as odd man out among his burdened brothers, we have 'Wayne (3), an easy-going toddler, affectionate and developing well.'

Finally another child, drawn from the bag at random and matching Wayne for untypical lack of personal complications, but carrying the uncertainty of his mother's schizophrenia into his unpredictable future. He is a boy of five, good-looking, intelligent, gently mannered and overtly comfortable in the world now, but who could present, in statistical terms, an above-average chance of developing schizophrenia during his late teens or early twenties. Who, then, would be willing to take that risk?

Of this quartet, numbers one, two and three labour under labelled disadvantages. John, at nine, is 'proud of his clothes and takes particular interest in his appearance'. Unusual and somehow sad. The retired rampager David, at six, 'takes an interest in his surroundings'; an odd statement when referring to most human beings over the age of six months, and which will need some clarification when would-be fosterers or adopters respond. And what, might be asked, would be a reasonable prognosis for the possibilities of any academic achievements? With the greater part of *bona fide* adopters stating that they would prefer an average or bright child – indeed, some will categorically insist that they can only consider a child with good educational prospects – children like poor David, already described as a potential second-rater, would most likely only be able to worm his way into a heart and home by way of introductory fostering. The same must be said of Fred, who the authorities admit may not be very bright and who, judging by the curiously telescoped phraseology, would seem to possess a unique interdependence between heart and teeth.

So quite apart from those children who, for reasons of obvious mental and/or physical handicap, find themselves lagging in the adoption stakes, there are those whose question-marks regarding their futures act as a deterrent. Denied the chance to settle into what could be negatively termed less disadvantaged homes, the majority of these children stand small hope of achieving them. That terrible phrase 'born to fail' sticks like a limpet. Prospective parents are afraid to take the plunge, reluctant to commit themselves to long odds without support or redress. Small beings, meanwhile, the dice already loaded against them, are caught in a Catch 22 situation.

Fostering, then, must be openly offered, realistically suggested, as a supported period of unrestricted duration, though with the possibility, not obligation, of taking full legal powers if and/or when the family feels confident enough to take-over on their own.

Alone? Well, often not quite. With these adoptions begotten out of fostering, some contact between child and natural parents, child and siblings, even child and grandparents, can constitute a condition of adoption. Although this idea may seem alien to the concept of adoption and detrimental to the cohesion expected of a nuclear family, access to early ties and affections need not split the child's loyalties or confuse the issue so long as it is handled properly.

Visits two or three times a year are often considered to be adequate, slowly severing the tie which will probably become no more than a formality or may even evaporate altogether over the years. Absence from the child does not, contrary to popular myth, make the heart grow fonder or at least not in the long term. It creates a distance quite separate from geography and is analogous to the healing of mental and emotional scars after bereavement.

There may be a time when a foster parent is invited to accept a child, sometimes a new baby, as a short-term pre-adoption placement. This infant settles in, wheedles itself into the very core of the family and, quite literally, identifies with it in every particular. Weeks, months drift by on a cloud of fulfilment only to be experienced within the magic circle of parenthood drawn from love. But take care; complacency blinds one to the harsh machinations of the rule book. The manoeuvres involved in preparing for an adoption can be long, difficult and punctuated by changes of decision which repeat themselves like regular traffic-lights. While the work is going on behind the scenes between what we are now required to call the 'Agency' and the candidates applying for an adoptive child, the fosterers are expected to carry on with the caring, expected to keep the metaphorical door ajar. However, in some protracted cases, especially where those fosterers rightly or wrongly consider the proceedings to be held up or dragging on under apparently insurmountable difficulties, a fierce possessiveness towards the baby takes over.

'Sharon,' writes Mrs B, 'came to us at six weeks old. She was a poor little mite. Didn't smile. Didn't seem to have much interest – only in her bottle. She was sore down below and had sticky eyes.' This 35-year-old woman, the mother of two school-children, had until this time seen her family as complete. However, over the twelve months of baby Sharon's stay, Mrs B had forged a bond with the child, was possessive, ready to fight with a real mother's tigerish intensity. She continues her letter, 'she's up for adoption isn't she? She's been here all these months and we've nursed her through, coaxed her on, given her everything we've got so she'll catch up and be a credit. They've taken all this time to find her a family, while we've done all the work. If it had turned out to be the matter of weeks which we'd expected, then it would have been different. But you take to a baby, look on it as your own after a while, and before you know where you are it's the be-all and end-all of your existence. We love Sharon. Can't they see that? We want to adopt her now so she won't have any changes, any upsets, and will just carry on with us as her family. But they won't let us.'

Personally I feel an extraordinarily strong sympathy for the B family. One does get attached to some children more than others; and one whom you have, so to speak, rescued by dint of loving care from a particularly sub-standard existence, somehow rests nearer the heart than any more robust howler. When, in addition to this intense mother-love, you have chosen to fight the original understanding that the apple of your eye was only taken in as a passing guest, the irresistible force has well and truly met the immovable object. Fuel is added to the Bs' argument because they argue that social services (the Agency) protracted Sharon's stay beyond the recognized short term of six months, failed to take the Bs' feelings into consideration and, above all, had dragged their feet in respect of the proposed adoption placement.

On top of all this, the Bs' stress that the transition from one couple of parents to another after almost fifteen months could be traumatically upsetting for Sharon.

The social worker in question, coping with a pretty heavy caseload, maintains that she has plodded on as efficiently as she could advertising far and wide – but has not as yet been able to report more than a few near misses. The basic problem is explained thus: the baby's mother is mentally retarded, has previously produced two other children, both of whom show a marked backwardness of development and who are in residential care. Would-be adopters, typically, show initial enthusiasm for Sharon herself, but then (as with the boy Wayne) pull out when her social history is divulged.

Currently Sharon is, thanks mainly to the devoted stimulation of the B family, a normal, middle-of-the-road infant. True, her mouth hangs open a bit and her reactions are not as sharp as Einstein's probably were in his second year, but she passes and has her quota of charm. But prospective adopters, particularly if they have taken independent counselling, and many seek this verification of motives, are aware that congenital retardation, in particular where the condition is acknowledged in other, and close, members of the same family, tends to become more apparent as time progresses.

The small baby, for instance, may be seen as a tiny bit behindhand; the 5-year-old, having been overtaken by his peers in, say, manipulative play and concentration span, can be judged as needing a wee bit more time to catch up; but by the time the child is ten or eleven, and possibly three or four years behind on the three R's, then the intelligence gap is really noticeable. The older the child, the wider the discrepancy between normal/average progress and that of a child with less spark. And people tend to plan ahead in connection with their progeny.

Perhaps we have digressed momentarily from the case in question. But yes, it will be difficult for the Agency to find an adoptive home for Sharon; the easy, and to the B couple the logical, placement would be achieved by simply leaving the baby where she is, let the desired legalities go through and close the case book. On the other hand the social workers concerned with planning feel that in the interests of the child she ought to be brought up in a family at some considerable distance from the birth family. The Bs live only a mile and a half away from her birth family. The temptation, later, for both Sharon and her first relatives to make contact could become overwhelming. Their somewhat shady reputation in the locality could rebound on the little girl. Embarrassment to the adopting family could adversely affect stability within it.

Taking the long view I'd be prepared to bet that the likely outcome would be a further protracted period of fostering, occasionally punctuated with hopes of likely takers, while the fosterers remain subject to anxiety and keep fighting for possession.

Possibly this may result in bad feeling between the Bs and the Agency, yet in all probability the situation will drift into one of long-term fostering. Conceivably, the Bs will generate enough energy to push for adoption after the statutory period of five years. They may just be willing to move house to another area in order to comply with official feelings. It has been done before; parents – and the Bs are, in every practical matter and from the baby's point of view, the parents – will move both molehills and mountain ranges to attain security in law.

There is a hardcore of parents and singles who care not a whit about the social/medical/mental/criminal background of any given child. If a living being needs a home – be it surplus gerbil, despondent underdog or child stuck in the regular pipeline – then the door and all within are made available. Here and there throughout the country one finds extraordinary and generally very chaotic families of almost infinite size where the ability to recite the multiplication tables or to teeter along the garden wall with a tennis ball on the end of the nose is not a condition of entry. Some of these families, to secure a future for succeeding generations of children, have set up Trusts which are administered for the benefit of the household concerned, and which hold valuable tax advantages. Such families are highly acclaimed by those Agencies which have had the good fortune to 'lose a child' to them.

However, far more usual is the modest addition of one or two, regardless of handicap, as a continuation of an existing family. Almost invariably this means that parents are extending years when they are tied. Sometimes, where a new child is severely hampered, a late adoption might entail caring for so long that retirement is out of the question. Yet some do it.

Half a dozen or so Agencies (apart from others which inevitably have their quota of the difficult-to-place) exist which concern themselves only with parents and children who fall into this special category. An adopter of this calibre would rarely be allowed to plunge into irrevocable legalities before a probationary period, for want of a better phrase, has been worked through. A child with extreme mental or physical difficulties needs more time to adapt to a fresh lifestyle; so do the new parents.

Opening a file at random I find 'T is mentally handicapped, and has occasional epileptic fits. She spends a lot of time examining little pieces of paper or just looking into space. She doesn't say much, but will sometimes hum a tune. She needs the constant attention of one or two parents to allow her to develop fully.'

'As C grows older his special needs will become more obvious. He will probably require remedial education and will never be able to live independently.'

'M lives at a school for children with emotional and behavioural difficulties. He is immature and doesn't always act sensibly, is quite isolated and has few friendships. He has been in trouble for stealing and gluesniffing.'

'L's development is causing some concern as, at one year old, she cannot yet sit up. She may also be mentally retarded.'

'J has severe learning difficulties and also needs a good deal of physical care. He cannot walk but it is believed that he will grow both emotionally and intellectually.'

Apart from these children, ranging right across the spectrum of childhood from infancy to mid-teens, there are two other groups which feature obviously on the lists of more unusual adoption-through-fostering situations. Youngsters who, simply because they have come into care after the age of, say, eleven or twelve, and are beyond that appealing and malleable stage of early childhood, are in effect presenting themselves as individuals in their own right. They bring with them a pattern of life which, from each side of any proposed union, might need diligent attention. Initially they seem to come in more as guests, though they understand that the intention is for them to stay permanently. This creates a curious situation for them to assimilate at one of the most emotionally pressured times in anyone's life. But remember, there are many teenagers on the lists and adopters have the satisfaction of knowing that these young people have, unlike the younger children, lent their own weight in the decision to go for adoption.

Consider for instance, 14-year-old A. 'A friendly, sociable boy with lots of friends. He enjoys art and is particularly good at drawing. He likes computer games, Kung Fu and football, is popular with adults and always has a girl-friend. He responds well to firmness and consistency and needs a family who will be able to provide this. After four years in a children's home he is himself very anxious to find a family of his own.'

Or 15-year-old P, who has 'had an unhappy year and has been unable to settle down in her children's home because she needs the adult attention that only a family can give. Although she looks quite grown-up she says she feels like a little girl most of the time. She would like to find parents with a very young child whom she could help to look after.'

The second typical adoption-through-fostering group falling outside those who are overtly handicapped are those children who come in multiples. Families of two, three, four, sometimes five or more, coming into care simultaneously or closely staggered, very often have a real and urgent need to be kept together. When there is no conceivable hope of their being kept together in their natural home, a new family could well provide the patience and skill required to repair the damage.

183

'M and N, normal, healthy sisters of four and six, need an adoptive family where they can be the youngest or only children. M is helpful and capable, tries hard to please and often sounds like a little woman. N is less outgoing and competes for attention. Both girls need firm guidelines, reassurance and encouragement.'

More difficult are 'T, Y and W, who are aged eleven, thirteen and fourteen and have been with foster parents for the past eighteen months. It has now been established that they will never return home, so a long-term arrangement would be in their interest. T tends to be moody at times, while Y is more temperamental and W of a quieter and more sensitive nature. All three boys have had a disrupted and confused life prior to their parents' separation and real stability would be the prime requisite of their new family.'

Parents who fall below the millionaire bracket might well blench at the thought of taking on such numbers simultaneously. Love, good intentions and an enormous house do not, alas, keep children fed, clothed and provided with 365 batteries a year for Walkman, computer games, torches and mobile monsters. With the change of status from fosterer to adopter the parent is automatically the recipient of the Child Benefit – though the loser of the maintenance sums paid for fostering by the authorities. On average that cuts the sum payable for the individual child to roughly one-sixth of that received while he was in care. In many instances, more especially if the newly-adopted child is particularly expensive to keep on account of, say, severe handicap, the presiding judge will arrange with the relevant authority for an agreed allowance to be kept up so that the standard of care can be maintained without financial hardship. In such a case the right to Attendance and Mobility Allowances will also be taken into account.

In short, so long as the heart is willing, the determination well sharpened and there is approval from all parties, then the fact that the family's bank account is modest need not preclude the adoption of a child.

Since the tail-end of 1985 there has been a legal halfway-house (between full adoption and the uncertainty of fostering) known as Custodianship, which in many situations suits both sets of parents and the child admirably. Though, as with adoption through the courts, this gives long-term security and considerably more rights, it is not as irrevocably binding as adoption. Maintenance payments may also be made to custodians at the discretion of the magistrate hearing the case.

Briefly, a fostering situation may be transformed into one of Custodianship, a) after a period of twelve months' continuous caring at the applicants' (or applicant's) address, but with the consent of those holding parental rights whether natural parent(s) or local authority as the case may be; or b) after a period of continuous care lasting over three years with or without the permission, blessing or cooperation of the erstwhile string-holders.

In Custodianship, the child's surname is not automatically changed, though in fact a change of surname may be effected with the agreement of all parties – the Custodian and the natural parents. If the child in question is old enough to make his own decision, then his wishes must be respected.

Statutory visits and other such obligations by the social services towards a fostered child cease with Custodianship, unless the new parents request continuation. They might for instance seek support in cases of baffling behavioural problems or handicap. All matters concerning choice of schools, training for careers, medical and para-medical treatment, all the normal decisions which mothers and fathers make on behalf of their offspring every day of the year now rest with the custodians. Where a parent's signature is called for (passport, permission for anaesthetic/surgery, sanction for marriage if under eighteen) a Custodian's will serve.

185

Older men and women, anxious to bring up a child as their own, yet unwilling to burden their grown-up sons or daughters with the care of, say, a handicapped teenager or young adult, will opt for Custodianship. In the event of the parents' death before the child reaches his majority, or if that child of whatever age is unable to live independently, no obligation is passed on to the next generation.

Couples or singles, then, who really do feel able to offer parenthood but who do not meet, initially, the very stringent guidelines set down by current vetting procedures need not dismiss their submission out of hand. Those who are already fostering may, with every advantage, go for a more permanent relationship, either in connection with a child already in their long-term care or with a separate application. Those who perhaps are not seen as ideal are, nevertheless, perfectly at liberty to approach their local social services to take on fostering with a view to adoption or custodianship. If a first application doesn't succeed, then boldly apply to one of the specialist agencies which are listed at the end of this book. Sympathetic consideration is given to all enquirers, even to those who might imagine they are not anything like the stereotype adoptive parents. However, we are not in this case discussing stereotype children, are we?

Some useful addresses

National Foster Care Association, Francis House, Francis Street, London SW1P 1DE.
Membership open to carers and professionals. Queries dealt with, including legal advice. Training, seminars and conferences organized. Quarterly magazine with strong 'families sought' content. Wide range of literature on all aspects of fostering.

National Children's Bureau, 8 Wakley Street, London EC1V 7QE.
Individual or corporate membership. In the main a research and development organization dealing with welfare, education and law, with a special interest in children under five. A broad list of lectures and discussions and an excellent information/library facility. Publishes *Who Cares?*, a journal compiled by those who have been or are currently 'in care'.

British Agencies for Adoption and Fostering, 11 Southwark Street, London SE1 1RQ.
Regional offices throughout Britain to offer help and information on fostering, adoption and fostering-view-to-adoption. Many useful leaflets. Training, counselling, placement work and consultancy.

Parent to Parent Information on Adoption Service, Lower Boddington, Near Daventry, Northamptonshire NN11 6YB.
Support and information for those contemplating/experiencing fostering-view-to-adoption. Starter pack free on request. Thereafter membership brings regular newsletter and profiles of children needing families.